SHARON JAYNES

THE
POWER
OF A
WOMAN'S
WORDS

HARVEST HOUSE PUBLISHERS
EUGENE, OREGON

Cover by Garborg Design Works, Savage, Minnesota

THE POWER OF A WOMAN'S WORDS
Copyright © 2007 by Sharon Jaynes
Published by Harvest House Publishers
Eugene, Oregon 97402
www.harvesthousepublishers.com

Library of Congress Cataloging-in-Publication Data
Jaynes, Sharon.
    The power of a woman's words / Sharon Jaynes.
        p. cm.
    ISBN 978-0-7369-1869-5 (pbk.)
    ISBN 978-0-7369-3502-9 (eBook)

    1. Influence (Psychology)—Religious aspects—Christianity. 2. Oral communication—Religious aspects—Christianity. 3. Christian women—Conduct of life. I. Title.
    BV4597.53.I52J39 2007
    248.8'43—dc22

                                                                      2007007378

Printed in the United States of America

16 17 18 19 20 / VP-SK / 22 21 20 19 18

To my precious friend Cynthia Price,
a woman who uses her words well.

Cynthia,
Many friends may come and go,
But rare the whole life through,
Are those who are forever friends,
Like the friend I've found in you.

Acknowledgments

Just as a painting combines many colors on a canvas to create what the artist intended, this manuscript combines many lives to create a portrait of *The Power of a Woman's Words*. I am so thankful for Jean Harper, Gayle Wentling, Catherine Grimes, Mary Marshal Young, Connie Roads, Gayle Roper, Glynnis Whitwer, Don and Jona Wright, Nancy Anderson, Mary Southerland, Bonnie Schulte, Mary Johnson, LeAnn Rice, Ginny Carlson, Larry Clark, and Kim Moore for sharing your stories of how you were impacted by a woman's words. The examples you shared help us all to see the impact our words have on those around us.

I am forever grateful to the staff of Harvest House Publishers. It is such an honor to work with this incredible team of men and women who truly are bringing in a harvest for God. Thank you, Bob Hawkins Jr., Terry Glaspey, and LaRae Weikert, for believing in the project; and Kim Moore for her expertise in editing.

And to my Girlfriends in God, Mary Southerland and Gwen Smith—I am so thankful that God has joined us together for such a time as this to share not only our words but our lives as well.

While this book is about the power of a woman's words, it is the power of a man's words that has been the wind beneath my wings along this entire journey. Thank you, Steve, my wonderful husband, for giving me the encouragement I've needed, for believing in me, and for praying for me each step of the way.

I am also so thankful for my son, Steven, an amazing young man whom God has used as a reflector of my words.

Finally, and most importantly, I am so thankful to my Savior, Jesus Christ. It is only by God's grace that I am allowed to reach out to His children by the written word. To God be the glory!

Contents

The
Power
We
Possess

MIXED MESSAGES

Discretion of speech is more than eloquence.

—FRANCIS BACON

MY FRIEND CATHERINE AND I set out for a lazy summer stroll through the neighborhood just before the fireflies emerged to celebrate the setting of the sun. We chatted about raising boys, working husbands, and decorating dilemmas. When we arrived back at her house, she invited me to come in and look at some fabric swatches for a new sofa. Before I knew it, a few minutes had turned into a few hours.

"Oh, my!" I exclaimed. "It's ten o'clock. I've been gone for over two hours! I bet Steve's worried sick. He doesn't even know where I am. I'd better give him a call before I start back home."

When I dialed our number, the answering machine picked up. After I listened to my sweet Southern greeting, I left a bitter message.

"Steve, I was calling to let you know I'm at Catherine's. I thought you'd be worried, but apparently you don't even care because you won't even pick up the phone!" Click. I said my goodbyes to Catherine and left feeling dejected. "I'm wandering around in the dark all alone and he doesn't even care," I mumbled to no one in particular.

As my eyes adjusted to the darkness, I noticed someone coming toward me. It was Sir Galahad riding on his steed...his bicycle!

"Where have you been?" Steve desperately asked. "I've been riding all over the neighborhood looking for you! Do you know what time it is?"

"Oh, you do care," I said with a grin, giving him a big hug.

"What are you talking about?"

"Oh, nothing. Let's go home."

When we arrived at the house, I quickly erased the message on the machine before Steve could hear my reprimanding words. *Whew,* I thought. *That was close.*

A few days later, Steve called me from work.

"Sharon, have you listened to the answering machine lately?"

"No, why?"

"Well, I think there's something on there you need to hear."

We hung up and I reached for my cell phone to call my home phone. The message on the answering machine went something like this.

(The voice of a sweet Southern belle) "Hello, you've reached the Jaynes' residence. We're unable to answer the phone right now... (enter the voice of Cruella De Vil) "I was calling to let you know I'm at Catherine's. I thought you'd be worried, but apparently you don't even care because you won't even pick up the phone!" (Return of sweet Southern belle) "At the sound of the beep, leave a message and we'll get back with you as soon as possible." Beep.

"Oh, my goodness!" I screamed. "How did this happen! How many people have heard this over the past three days?"

I called the phone company, and they explained that sometimes during a thunderstorm (which had occurred three days prior), lightning strikes the wires and answering machine messages get scrambled. My message somehow became attached to the greeting.

I was mortified. It sounded like Dr. Jekyll and Mrs. Hyde.

"Lord," I prayed, "this is so embarrassing."

"Yes, it is," He replied.

Well, He didn't really *say* that in so many words. It was more like this: "With the tongue we praise our Lord and Father, and with it we curse men, who have been made in God's likeness. Out of the same mouth come praise and cursing. My brothers and sisters, this should not be. Can both fresh water and salt water flow from the same spring? My brothers and sisters, can a fig tree bear olives, or a grapevine bear figs? Neither can a salt spring produce fresh water" (James 3:9-12 TNIV).

"Okay, Lord, I get the message." But, unfortunately, so did a lot of other people.

I am amazed how quickly we women can flit back and forth between blessing and belittling, praising and putting down, cheering and critiquing—all in a matter of seconds. God has given us incredible power in our sphere of influence, and it begins with the words we speak. Few forces have as powerful an effect as the sounds that pass our lips. Our words can spark a child to accomplish great feats, encourage a husband to conquer the world, fan the dying embers of a friend's broken dreams into flame, encourage a fellow believer to run the race set before her, and draw a lost soul to Christ.

> *A word is dead when it is said, some say. I say it just begins to live that day.*
>
> EMILY DICKINSON

I invite you to explore one of the mysteries of the feminine mystique—the power of a woman's words. In addition to looking at how our words impact those we come in contact with every day, we'll also look at various women in the Bible and how their words influenced generations after them. We'll explore the power available to each of us to harness this mighty force and use it for good. Most importantly, we'll join hands and hearts and discover how to change the words we speak to become the women God intended all along.

Are words powerful? Yes! Just how powerful? We'll learn together. Let's take a look at one of God's most incredible gifts to mankind and consider the potential we have right under our noses...words.

A careless word may kindle strife;

A cruel word may wreck a life.

A bitter word may hate instill;

A brutal word may smite and kill.

A gracious word may smooth the way;

A joyous word may light the day.

A timely word may lessen stress;

A loving word may heal and bless.

AUTHOR UNKNOWN

God's Incredible Gift

*The Bible has a lot to say about our mouths,
our lips, our tongues, for our speech betrays us.
What is down in the well will come up in the bucket.*

—Vance Havner

GOD HAS GIVEN us an incredible treasure—this gift of words. But the gift wasn't meant to be hoarded or ill used. The gift is to be opened and shared to help others be all that God intended them to be. Miss Thompson, a school teacher who taught fifth grade, saw firsthand how an encouraging word can change the course of a day...the course of a life. Here's her story:

Three Letters from Teddy

Teddy's letter came today and now that I've read it, I will place it in my cedar chest with the other things that are important to my life.

"I wanted you to be the first to know."

I smiled as I read the words he had written, and my heart swelled with a pride that I had no right to feel. *Teddy Stallard.* I have not seen Teddy Stallard since he was a student in my fifth-grade class, fifteen years ago.

I'm ashamed to say that from the first day he stepped into my classroom, I disliked Teddy. Teachers try hard not to have favorites in a class, but we try even harder not to show dislike for a child, any child.

Nevertheless, every year there are one or two children that one cannot help but be attached to, for teachers are human, and it is human nature to like bright, pretty, intelligent people, whether they are ten years old or twenty-five. And sometimes, not too often fortunately, there will be one or two students to whom the teacher just can't seem to relate.

I had thought myself quite capable of handling my personal feelings along that line until Teddy walked into my life. There wasn't a child I particularly liked that year, but Teddy was most assuredly one I disliked.

He was a dirty little boy. Not just occasionally, but all the time. His hair hung low over his ears, and he actually had to hold it out of his eyes as he wrote his papers in class. (And this was before it was fashionable to do so!) Too, he had a peculiar odor about him that I could never identify.

Yes, his physical faults were many, but his intellect left a lot to be desired. By the end of the first week I knew he was hopelessly behind the others. Not only was he behind, he was just plain slow! I began to withdraw from him immediately.

Any teacher will tell you that it's more of a pleasure to teach a bright child. It is definitely more rewarding for one's ego. But any teacher worth his or her credentials can channel work to the bright child, keeping that child challenged and learning, while the major effort is with the slower ones. Any teacher *can* do this. Most teachers *do,* but I didn't. Not that year.

In fact, I concentrated on my best students and let the others follow along as best they could. Ashamed as I am to admit it, I took perverse pleasure in using my red pen; and each time I came to Teddy's papers, the cross-marks (and they were many) were always a little larger and a little redder than necessary.

"Poor work!" I would write with a flourish.

While I did not actually ridicule the boy, my attitude was obviously quite apparent to the class, for he quickly became the class "goat," the outcast—the unlovable and the unloved.

He knew I didn't like him, but he didn't know why. Nor did I know—then or now—why I felt such an intense dislike for him. All I know is that he was a little boy no one cared about, and I made no effort on his behalf.

The days rolled by and we made it through the Fall Festival, the Thanksgiving holidays, and I continued marking happily with my red pen. As our Christmas break approached, I knew that Teddy would never catch up in time to be promoted to the sixth-grade level. He would be a repeater.

To justify myself, I went to his cumulative folder from time to time. He had very low grades for the first four years, but no grade failure. How he had made it, I didn't know. I closed my mind to the personal remarks:

First Grade: "Teddy shows promise by work and attitude, but he has a poor home situation."

Second Grade: "Teddy could do better. Mother terminally ill. He receives little help at home."

Third Grade: "Teddy is a pleasant boy. Helpful, but too serious. Slow learner. Mother passed away end of the year."

Fourth Grade: "Very slow but well behaved. Father shows no interest."

Well, they passed him four times, but he will certainly repeat fifth grade! Do him good! I said to myself.

And then the last day before the holidays arrived. Our little tree on the reading table sported paper and popcorn chains. Many gifts were heaped underneath, waiting for the big moment.

Teachers always get several gifts at Christmas, but mine that year seemed bigger and more elaborate than ever. There was not a student who had not brought me one. Each unwrapping brought squeals of delight and the proud giver would receive effusive thank-yous.

His gift wasn't the last one I picked up. In fact it was in the middle of the pile. Its wrapping was a brown paper bag, and he had colored Christmas trees and red bells all over it. It was stuck together with masking tape. "For Miss Thompson—From Teddy."

The group was completely silent and I felt conspicuous, embarrassed because they all stood watching me unwrap that gift. As I removed the last bit of masking tape, two items fell to my desk. A gaudy rhinestone bracelet with several stones missing and a small bottle of dime-store cologne—half empty. I could hear the snickers and whispers, and I wasn't sure I could look at Teddy.

"Isn't this lovely?" I asked, placing the bracelet on my wrist. "Teddy, would you help me fasten it?"

He smiled shyly as he fixed the clasp, and I held up my wrist for all of them to admire. There were a few hesitant *ooh's* and *ahh's*, but, as I dabbed the cologne behind my ears, all the little girls lined up for a dab behind their ears.

I continued to open the gifts until I reached the bottom of the pile. We ate our refreshments until the bell rang. The children filed out with shouts of "See you next year!" and "Merry Christmas!" but Teddy waited at his desk.

When they had all left, he walked toward me clutching his gift and books to his chest.

"You smell just like Mom," he said softly. "Her bracelet looks real pretty on you, too. I'm glad you liked it."

He left quickly and I locked the door, sat down at my desk and wept, resolving to make up to Teddy what I had deliberately deprived him of—a teacher who cared.

I stayed every afternoon with Teddy from the day class resumed on January 2 until the last day of school. Sometimes we worked together. Sometimes he worked alone while I drew up lesson plans or graded papers. Slowly but surely he caught up with the rest of the class. Gradually there was a definite upward curve in his grades.

He did not have to repeat the fifth grade. In fact, his final averages were among the highest in the class, and although I knew he would be moving out of the state when school was out, I was not worried for him. Teddy had reached a level that would stand him in good stead the following year, no matter where he went. He had enjoyed a measure of success, and as we were taught in our education courses: "Success builds success."

I did not hear from Teddy until several years later when his first letter appeared in my mailbox.

> *Dear Miss Thompson,*
>
> *I just wanted you to be the first to know. I will be graduating second in my class on May 25 from E_____ High School.*
>
> *Very truly yours,*
>
> *Teddy Stallard*

I sent him a card of congratulations and a small package, a pen and pencil set. I wondered what he would do after graduation. I found out four years later when Teddy's second letter came.

> *Dear Miss Thompson,*
>
> *I was just informed today that I'll be graduating first in my class. The university has been a little tough but I'll miss it.*
>
> *Very truly yours,*
>
> *Teddy Stallard*

I sent him a good pair of sterling silver monogrammed cuff links and a card, so proud of him I could burst!

And now—today—Teddy's third letter:

> *Dear Miss Thompson,*
>
> *I wanted you to be the first to know. As of today I am Theodore J. Stallard, MD. How about that???!!!*
>
> *I'm going to be married on July 27, and I'm hoping you can come and sit where Mom would sit if she were here. I'll have no family there as Dad died last year.*
>
> > *Very truly yours,*
> >
> > *Ted Stallard*

I'm not sure what kind of gift one sends to a doctor on completion of medical school. Maybe I'll just wait and take a wedding gift, but the note can't wait.

> *Dear Ted,*
>
> *Congratulations! You made it and you did it yourself! In spite of those like me and not because of us, this day has come for you.*
>
> *God bless you. I'll be at that wedding with bells on!!!*[1]

Miss Thompson changed the course of one little boy's life. She gave Teddy words that built him up when he felt as though life had knocked him down for good. Can't you hear her now? "Great job, Teddy!" "You can do it!" She became the wind beneath his wings when he felt as though he had been grounded from flight. And years later, she had a front row seat as she watched him soar into his future. That is the power of a woman's words. An incredible gift God has given those created in His very image.

An Incredible Gift

"In the beginning God created the heavens and the earth"

(Genesis 1:1). That seems like a splendid place for us to start our journey—at the beginning of time. When God created the world and stocked the seas with marine life and the skies with winged creatures—when He caused the stars to ignite the night sky and placed the sun to light the day and the moon to illumine the darkness—He did so with words. *"And God said,* 'Let there be light.'" *"And God said,* 'Let there be an expanse between the waters to separate water from water.'" *"And God said,* 'Let the water under the sky be gathered to one place, and let dry ground appear.'" *"And God said,* 'Let there be lights in the expanse of the sky to separate the day from the night.'" *"And*

> *In the beginning was the Word, and the Word was with God, and the Word was God.*
>
> JOHN 1:1

God said, 'Let the water teem with living creatures, and let birds fly above the earth across the expanse of the sky.'" *"And God said,* 'Let the land produce living creatures according to their kinds.'" *"And God said,* 'Let us make man in our own image, in our likeness, and let them rule over the fish of the sea and the birds of the air, over the livestock, over all the earth, and over all the creatures that move along the ground.'" And it was so. (See Genesis 1:3-26.) God spoke and what was not became what is. When God created the heavens and the earth, He used a mighty force—words. "By the word of the LORD were the heavens made, their starry host by the breath of his mouth" (Psalm 33:6).

Amazingly, when God created mankind in His own image, He gave us that same powerful tool. He didn't entrust words to zebras, birds, monkeys, elephants, lizards, or horses. He entrusted words to mere mortals. Our words also have creative potential. They can create a smile on a discouraged child's face, lighten the heart of a husband loaded down with burdens, fan into a flame the dying embers of a friend's smoldering dreams, cheer brothers and sisters in Christ to run the race with endurance, and bring the message of the hope and healing of Jesus Christ to a wounded world. Our words become the mirror in which others see themselves. Words are one of the most powerful forces in the universe, and amazingly, God has entrusted them to you and me.

A Powerful Force

I've always been amazed at the power in a tiny atom too small to be seen by the naked eye. Fission (splitting the nucleus of an atom) and fusion (joining nuclei together) have the potential to generate enough power to provide energy for an entire city or enough destructive potential to level an entire town. It all depends on how and when the joining together or splitting apart takes place.

So it is with our words. Bound in one small group of muscles called the tongue lies an instrument with huge potential for good or evil, to build up or to tear down, to empower or devour, to heal or to hurt. It all depends on how and when the joining together and splitting apart take place. Our words can make or break a marriage, paralyze or propel a friend, sew together or tear apart a relationship, build up or bury a dream, curse God or confess Christ. With our tongues we defend or destroy, heal or kill, cheer or churn. And we, as women, seem to be quite talented at deciding when and where to wield this tiny sword.

> *Sticks and stones will break our bones, but words will break our hearts.*
> —ROBERT FULGHUM

Just as God used words to create physical life, our words can be the spark to generate spiritual life. Paul taught, "If you confess with your mouth, 'Jesus is Lord,' and believe in your heart that God raised him from the dead, you will be saved. For it is with your heart that you believe and are justified, and it is *with your mouth that you confess and are saved*" (Romans 10:9). Wow! It is with our mouth that we are saved. That is radical responsibility. That is potently powerful.

In the Bible, the book of James paints a poignant picture of the power of our words:

> When we put bits into the mouths of horses to make them obey us, we can turn the whole animal. Or take ships as an example. Although they are so large and are driven by strong winds, they are steered by a very small rudder wherever the pilot wants to go. Likewise, the tongue is a small part of the body, but it makes great boasts. Consider what a great forest is set on fire by a small spark. The tongue also is a fire, a world of evil among the parts of the body. It corrupts the whole person, *sets the whole course of his life on fire,* and is itself set on fire by hell (James 3:3-6).

On average, 4.3 million acres of forests are destroyed by wildfires each year in the United States.[2] In 2000, nearly 123,000 separate fires destroyed 8.5 million acres of forest. About half are destroyed by natural causes, such as lightning strikes, and the rest are caused by the carelessness of mankind. While forest fires leave naked trees and barren hillsides that take years to revive, lives singed by fiery words can be laid bare forever. We would never carelessly fling a lit match out of a car window while passing a national forest, and yet many times we carelessly toss fiery words about as we pass through life.

The writer of Proverbs notes, "Death and life are in the power of the tongue" (Proverbs 18:21 NASB). Of all the spiritual disciplines, I believe bringing our tongues under the submission of the Holy Spirit is one of the greatest. Why? Because through our words we bring death and through our words we bring life. They take us out to stormy seas and lead us into tranquil waters.

There is a story told about Xanthus the philosopher. He once told his servant he was going to have some friends for dinner the following evening and instructed him to get the best thing he could find in the market. When the philosopher and his guests sat down the next day at the table, they had nothing but tongue—four or five courses of tongue cooked in various ways. The philosopher finally lost his patience and said to his servant, "Didn't I tell you to get the best thing in the market?" The servant said, "I did get the best thing in the market. Isn't the tongue the organ of sociability, the organ of eloquence, the organ of kindness, the organ of worship?"

Then Xanthus said, "Tomorrow I want you to get the worst thing in the market." The next day when the philosopher sat at the table, there was nothing but tongue—four or five courses of tongue— tongue in this shape and in that shape. The philosopher lost his patience again and said, "Didn't I tell you to get the worst thing in the market?" The servant replied, "I did; for isn't the tongue the organ of blasphemy, the organ of defamation, the organ of lying?"[3]

With words we govern men.

—BENJAMIN DISRAELI

I have never eaten tongue before, but I have had to eat my words. While words are one of God's most incredible gifts, in the wrong hands, or rather wrong mouth, they posses destructive potential.

A Desperate Need

One day I was glancing through an insert in my local newspaper called *The Mecklenburg Neighbor*. A calendar of events for the week was listed on the last two pages. Entry after entry mentioned support group meetings: Adoptive Parents Support Group, Adult Children of Alcoholics Support Group, Alzheimer's Disease Support Group, Dementia Caregivers Support Group, Amputee Support Group, Breast-feeding Support Group, Codependents Anonymous, Eating Disorders Anonymous, Emotions Anonymous, Gamblers Anonymous, Headaches Anonymous, Moms of Multiples, Sex Addicts Anonymous…All in all, 146 support group meetings were scheduled in my fair city in one week. A boxed message was posted above the upper-right-hand column: "If you are looking for a support group not mentioned here, give us a call and we'll find one for you."

I closed the newspaper with a knot in the pit of my stomach. How desperately men and women long for an encouraging word. They need a cheerleader to tell them, "You can do it. Don't give up!" They long for a fellow journeyman to bolster them up when the road is too arduous to travel alone. They yearn for teammates to rally behind them, reminding them they are not isolated in this game called life.

Years ago there were no such things as support groups. Rather, we had family or neighbors who helped when burdens became too difficult to bear alone. Women talked over the fence as they raised children together. They canned vegetables together when the crops came in. They stitched quilts to keep bodies warm and chatted to keep their hearts warm. But times have changed. Many of us don't even know our next-door neighbors' names, our families live across several state lines, and we've lost that sense of community that was the mainstay just a few generations ago. Where once we had a welcome mat at our front doors, now we have warning stickers to let those who approach our homes know we have an alarm system. And if you're like me, you have both welcome and warning.

This lack of community is prevalent in our Christian community as well. A few years ago I was in a couples' Bible study. One man in the group had only been a Christian for a short time. "You know what I miss most since I became a Christian?" he asked. "I miss the bars. I miss talking with other men."

His confession broke my heart. Rob didn't miss the alcohol. He missed the fellowship where no one would judge, condemn, nag, discourage, or tear him down. The bar was a safe place. I read something a few years ago that reminded me of Rob's lament:

> The neighborhood bar is possibly the best counterfeit there
> is to the fellowship Christ wants to give His church. It's an
> imitation, dispensing liquor instead of grace, escape rather

than reality, but it's permissive, accepting, and inclusive fellowship. It is unshockable. It is democratic. You can tell people secrets and they usually don't tell others or even want to. The bar flourishes not because most people are alcoholics, but because God has put into the human heart the desire to know and be known, to love and be loved, and so many seek a counterfeit at the price of a few beers."[4]

Why do spouses stop by the neighborhood bar before heading home? Could it be the same reason teenagers prefer peers over parents, the same reason church hoppers bounce from one church to the next, or the same reason hurting people attend support groups instead of sharing their struggles among friends? Could it be they are looking for a safe harbor, an uplifting word, a verbal pat on the back—grace for the grumpy, safety for the storm-tossed, and rest for the bone-weary? I've never met anyone yet who didn't need a kind word. People need a place where they can set anchor without fear of pirates coming aboard and robbing them blind. I believe we can be that "safe place." We can learn to speak words of grace that invite those around us to come ashore for a needed respite and then set sail once the storm has passed.

A Simple Choice

We are shaped by words from those who love us or refuse to love us. We are shaped by the words of those who don't even know our names. It is the heart cry of all mankind to be loved and accepted, and sometimes a simple word of encouragement can make all the difference.

William Barclay said, "One of the highest of human duties is the duty of encouragement. It is easy to laugh at men's ideals; it is easy to pour cold water on their enthusiasm; it is easy to discourage others. The world is full of discouragers. We have a Christian duty to encourage one another. Many a time a word of praise or thanks or appreciation or cheer has kept a man on his feet. Blessed is the man [or woman] who speaks such a word."[5]

What exactly is encouragement? My dictionary defines it "to give courage or confidence to; to raise the hopes of; to help on by sympathetic advice and interest, to advise and make it easy for [someone to do something] to promote or stimulate; to strengthen." In contrast, discouragement is "to say or take away the courage of, to deter, to lessen enthusiasm for and so restrict or hinder."

Amazingly, our words have the capacity for both, and we are faced with the choice every time we speak as to which it will be. The Hebrew word for "mouth," *peh,* is often translated "edge." Like a knife, the tongue has a sharp, powerful edge that can either be used to heal or destroy. A knife in the hands of a skilled surgeon brings healing and life, but a knife in the hands of a felon brings death and destruction. Like the surgeon, we can study how to use our mouths to bring life to those around us. But it's not easy, and the tongue is difficult to control.

Our words should build up and not tear down. They should minister grace or, as one little girl explained to Florence Littauer during a children's sermon, "be like silver boxes with bows on top." They should be verbal presents. They are God's gift to us, and we in turn give them as gifts to those around us. But words are not ordinary presents. They are often displayed on a prominent shelf in the heart as a treasured possession.

A Treasured Keepsake

How long do words linger in someone's heart? How far-reaching are the echoes of a kind word? I believe the impact of a spoken or written word can remain long after our bodies have left this earth. Marie learned the lasting impact of words from a group of her students. Here is her story:

> He was in the first third-grade class I taught at Saint Mary's School in Morris, Minnesota. All thirty-four of my students were dear to me, but Mark Eklund was one in a million. Very neat in appearance, he had that happy-to-be-alive attitude that made even his occasional mischievousness delightful.

Mark also talked incessantly. I had to remind him again and again that talking without permission was not acceptable. What impressed me so much, though, was his sincere response every time I had to correct him for misbehaving. "Thank you for correcting me, Sister!" I didn't know what to make of it at first, but before long I became accustomed to hearing it many times a day.

Jesus said, "Heaven and earth will pass away, but my words will not pass away."

MATTHEW 24:35

One morning my patience was growing thin when Mark talked once too often, and then I made a novice-teacher's mistake. I looked at Mark and said, "If you say one more word, I am going to tape your mouth shut!" It wasn't ten seconds later when Chuck blurted out, "Mark is talking again." I hadn't asked any of the students to help me watch Mark, but since I had stated the punishment in front of the class, I had to act on it.

I remember the scene as if it had occurred this morning. I walked to my desk, very deliberately opened the drawer, and took out a roll of masking tape. Without saying a word, I proceeded to Mark's desk, tore off two pieces of tape and made a big X with them over his mouth. I then returned to the front of the room.

As I glanced at Mark to see how he was doing, he winked at me. That did it! I started laughing. The class cheered as I walked back to Mark's desk, removed the tape, and shrugged my shoulders. His first words were, "Thank you for correcting me, Sister."

At the end of the year I was asked to teach junior high math. The years flew by, and before I knew it Mark was in my classroom again. He was more handsome than ever and just as polite. Since he had to listen carefully to my instruction in the "new math," he did not talk as much in ninth grade as he had in the third.

One Friday, things just didn't feel right. We had worked hard on a new concept all week, and I sensed that the students were growing frustrated with themselves and edgy with one another. I had to stop this crankiness before it got out of hand. So I asked them to list the names of the other students in the room on two sheets of paper, leaving a space between each name. Then I told them to think of the nicest thing they could say about each of their classmates and write it down.

It took the remainder of the class period to finish the assignment, and as the students left the room, each one handed me the papers. Charlie smiled. Mark said, "Thank you for teaching me, Sister. Have a good weekend."

That Saturday, I wrote down the name of each student on a separate sheet of paper, and I listed what everyone else had said about that individual. On Monday I gave each student his or her list. Before long, the entire class was smiling. "Really?" I heard whispered. "I never knew that meant anything to anyone!" "I didn't know others liked me so much!"

No one ever mentioned those papers in class again. I never knew if they discussed them after class or with their parents, but it didn't matter. The exercise had accomplished its purpose. The students were happy with themselves and with one another again.

That group of students moved on. Several years later, after I returned from vacation, my parents met me at the airport. As we were driving home, Mother asked the usual questions about the trip, the weather, my experiences in general. There was a slight lull in the conversation. Mother gave Dad a sideways glance and simply said, "Dad?" My father cleared his throat as he usually did before something important. "The Eklunds called last night," he began.

"Really?" I said. "I haven't heard from them in years. I wonder how Mark is."

Dad responded quietly. "Mark was killed in Vietnam," he said.

"The funeral is tomorrow, and his parents would like it if you could attend." To this day I can still point to the exact spot on I-494 where Dad told me about Mark.

I had never seen a serviceman in a military coffin before. Mark looked so handsome, so mature. All I could think at that moment was *Mark, I would give all the masking tape in the world if only you would talk to me.*

The church was packed with Mark's friends. Chuck's sister sang "The Battle Hymn of the Republic." Why did it have to rain on the day of the funeral? It was difficult enough at the graveside. The pastor said the usual prayers, and the bugler played "Taps." One by one those who loved Mark took a last walk by the coffin.

I was the last one. As I stood there, one of the soldiers who had acted as pallbearer came up to me. "Were you Mark's math teacher?" he asked. I nodded as I continued to stare at the coffin. "Mark talked about you a lot," he said.

After the funeral, most of Mark's former classmates headed to Chuck's farmhouse for lunch. Mark's mother and father were there, obviously waiting for me. "We want to show you something," his father said, taking a wallet out of his pocket. "They found this on Mark when he was killed. We thought you might recognize it."

Opening the billfold, he carefully removed two worn pieces of notebook paper that had obviously been taped, folded, and refolded many times. I knew without looking that the papers were the ones on which I had listed all the good things each of Mark's classmates had said about him. "Thank you so much for doing that," Mark's mother said. "As you can see, Mark treasured it."

Mark's classmates started to gather around us. Charlie smiled rather sheepishly and said, "I still have my list. It's in the top drawer of my desk at home." Chuck's wife said, "Chuck asked me to put his in our wedding album." "I have mine too," Marilyn said. "It's in my diary." Then Vicki, another classmate, reached into her pocketbook, took out her wallet, and showed her worn and frazzled list to the group. "I carry this with me at all times," Vicki said without batting an eyelash. "I think we all saved our lists."[6]

How long will our words echo in the hearts and minds of our children, our husbands, our friends, fellow believers, and the world? For all eternity, my friends. To the end of the age.

A *W*OMAN'S *A*MAZING *P*OTENTIAL

*There is no more noble occupation in the world
than to assist another human being to succeed.*

—ALAN LOY McGINNIS

HAVE YOU EVER MET SOMEONE who just seems to take the wind out of your sails? You have a tiny spark of excitement, mention it to a friend, and then she aims the fire extinguishers of discouraging words right at your hopes and dreams and douses your enthusiasm.

Susan was walking with a friend and sharing about an incredible ministry experience she had on an airplane.

"I sat beside this young girl who had experienced so much trauma in her young life," Susan explained. "She had been abused as a child, neglected as a teen, and beaten by her boyfriend as a young adult. I know God placed us side by side on that flight. For two hours we talked, cried, and finally prayed together."

"Did you believe her?" the friend asked.

"Yes," Susan replied. "Why wouldn't I?"

"I don't know. I think sometimes people make up stories about their lives. Sometimes it's just too much to believe."

With those words Susan's soaring spirits began a slow descent.

Nothing makes a heart fly like bringing the hope and healing of Jesus Christ to a hurting world. Susan had experienced that first-hand. She was still breathing in the crisp air of her mountaintop experience when the words of a friend rolled in like a dark cloud and rained down discouraging words that made Susan run for shelter. If the girl had made up her story, then Susan was a fool and ministry did not take place at all. Her ministry had been for naught and her enthusiasm for sharing the gospel in the future was squelched.

> *People are failures, not because they are stupid, but because they are not sufficiently impassioned.*
>
> —BURT STRUTHERS

It's very easy to throw water on the fire of someone's enthusiasm. It's very easy to extinguish a dream. But I believe God wants us to be women who ignite the fire in another's heart rather than extinguish the flames.

Have you ever noticed that there are certain people who bring out the best in others, and then there are certain people who tend to bring out the worst? I've heard them referred to as "attic people" and "basement people." One lifts you up; the other pulls you down.

I can think of people who seem to be the peroxide of the soul. Within minutes in their presence, all the impurities in my heart begin bubbling to the surface. It is not so much that I don't like the person. I just don't like the person I become when I am around them.

On the other hand, there are women I love to be around because I like who I am when I am with them. They bring out the best in me. That sounds awfully selfish, doesn't it? But, honestly, who doesn't enjoy being around people who hold up an invisible mirror of acceptance and inspire us to be our best?

When we become women who expect the best in others and use our words to tell them so, they usually go to great lengths to meet our expectations. As women, we can determine to be gold miners who use our words to dig deep into a person's soul to unearth the treasures hidden below the surface. I have had such gold miners in my own life.

For most of my life I struggled with feelings of inferiority, insecurity, and inadequacy. But God sent various women with the hard hat of His love into my life to unearth treasures hidden beneath my protective shell. Mary Marshal Young helped me see who I really am as a child of God. She aimed the light of God's Word into the dark caverns of my soul to reveal the gold veins imbedded in the rocky crags of past hurts.

Gayle Roper read a few of my first stories and encouraged me not to give up on writing, even if I was met with rejection. "You have a gift," she said. "Don't give up when you are rejected. The difference between a writer and a published author is that the published author doesn't give up. You can do it. Press on!"

Ginny had the opposite experience with her mother. When she was ten years old, her father died. This was hard on her because she always thought of him as her protector. *Who will love me the way I am? Who will love me for me?*

Ginny's older sister and younger brother were smart kids; they made the honor roll all the time. "You're not as smart as your sister," her mother remarked. "You'll never make the honor roll."

"We live up or down to the expectations people place on us," Ginny told me. "I did not make the honor roll until after my mother died. I was fifteen when she passed away, and after that I made the honor roll every time. While I missed my mom, with her low estimation of me removed I could blossom and grow into the woman God had intended all along. No longer did her negative words keep me down."

Every individual believes deep down that he or she has a greater capacity for success than they are currently experiencing. They simply need someone who will believe in them and tell them so—someone who will fan the flame rather than extinguish the fire. We have that potential with our words.

The Wind Beneath Her Wings

Jean Harper had both encouragers and extinguishers in her life. Let's ponder her story as told by Jean and Carol Kline.

> In 1959, when Jean was in the third grade, her teacher gave the class an assignment to write a report on what they wanted to be when they grew up. Jean's father was a crop duster pilot in the little farming community in Northern California where she was raised, and Jean was totally captivated by airplanes and flying. She poured her heart into her report and included all of her dreams; she wanted to crop dust, make parachute jumps, seed clouds and be an airline pilot. Her paper came back with an "F" on it. The teacher told her it was a "fairy tale" and that none of the occupations she listed were women's jobs. Jean was crushed and humiliated.
>
> She showed her father the paper, and he told her that of course she could become a pilot. "Look at Amelia Earhart," he said. "That teacher doesn't know what she's talking about."
>
> But as the years went by, Jean was beaten down by the discouragement and negativity she encountered whenever she talked about her career—"Girls can't become airline pilots; never have, never will. You're not smart enough, you're crazy. That's impossible."—until finally Jean gave up.
>
> In her senior year of high school, her English teacher was a Mrs. Dorothy Slaton. Mrs. Slaton was an uncompromising, demanding teacher with high standards and a low tolerance for excuses. She refused to treat her students like children, instead expecting them to behave like the responsible adults they would have to be to succeed in the real world after graduation. Jean was scared of her at first but grew to respect her firmness and fairness.
>
> One day Mrs. Slaton gave the class an assignment. "What do you think you'll be doing ten years from now?" Jean thought about the assignment. *Pilot? No way. Flight attendant? I'm not pretty enough—they'd never accept me. Wife? What guy would want me? Waitress? I could do that.* That felt safe, so she wrote it down.

Mrs. Slaton collected the papers and nothing more was said. Two weeks later, the teacher handed back the assignments, face down on each desk, and asked this question: "If you had unlimited finances, unlimited access to the finest schools, unlimited talents and abilities, what would you do?" Jean felt a rush of the old enthusiasm, and with excitement she wrote down all her old dreams. When the students stopped writing, the teacher asked, "How many students wrote the same thing on both sides of the paper?" Not one hand went up.

The next thing that Mrs. Slaton said changed the course of Jean's life. The teacher leaned forward over her desk and said, "I have a little secret for you all. You do have unlimited abilities and talents. You *do* have access to the finest schools, and you *can* arrange for unlimited finances if you want something badly enough. This is it! When you leave school, if you don't go for your dreams, *no one* will do it for you. You can have what you want if you want it enough."

The hurt and fear of years of discouragement crumbled in the face of the truth of what Mrs. Slaton had said. Jean felt exhilarated and a little scared. She stayed after class and went up to the teacher's desk. Jean thanked Mrs. Slaton and told her about her dream of becoming a pilot. Mrs. Slaton half rose and slapped the desk top. "Then do it!" she said.

So Jean did. It didn't happen overnight. It took 10 years of hard work, facing opposition that ranged from quiet skepticism to outright hostility. It wasn't in Jean's nature to stand up for herself when someone refused or humiliated her; instead, she would quietly try to find another way.

She became a private pilot and then got the necessary ratings to fly air freight and even commuter planes, but always as a copilot. Her employers were openly hesitant about promoting her because she was a woman. Even her father advised her to try something else. "It's impossible," he said. "Stop banging your head against the wall!"

But Jean answered, "Dad, I disagree. I believe that things are going to change, and I want to be at the head of the pack when they do."

Jean went on to do everything her third grade teacher said was a fairy tale—she did some crop dusting, made a few hundred parachute jumps, and even seeded clouds for a summer season as a weather modification pilot. In 1978, she became one of the first three female pilot trainees ever accepted by United Airlines and one of only 50 women airline pilots in the nation at the time. Today, Jean Harper is a Boeing 737 captain for United.

It was the power of one well-placed positive word, one spark of encouragement from a woman Jean respected that gave that uncertain young girl the strength and faith to pursue her dream. Today Jean says, "I chose to believe her."[1]

The Wind Beneath Our Wings

Jesus was the Master of believing in the best in others and encouraging them to reach beyond their own limited view of their abilities. His disciples had witnessed Jesus command a lame man to walk, restore the rotting skin of a leprous outcast, remove fever from Peter's mother-in-law with a touch, calm a raging storm, deliver a man from demons, and raise a little girl from the dead. But Jesus wanted more from His friends than to remain spectators in the gospel. He longed for them to be participants and partakers.

On a spring day shortly after the Passover celebration, Jesus retreated to the north shore of the Sea of Galilee. However, crowds of people quickly pursued this miracle worker to witness His teaching and healing power. As the sun began to sink to the horizon, His disciples remarked that the people were growing hungry. Jesus turned to Philip and asked, "Where shall we buy bread for these people to eat?"

Jesus was not concerned with a lack of provisions. Rather, He was taking this opportunity to invite the disciples to share in His ministry. He didn't need their help. However, He wanted to invite them to participate in a miracle to boost their confidence and faith. It was a gentle breeze in their sails.

Philip was smart. In a matter of moments he calculated that it would take eight months' wages to feed the ten thousand people gathered on the hill. But Jesus wasn't looking for facts; He was looking for faith.

Andrew was practical. He canvassed the crowd to see what resources were available...and he came back with five small barley cakes and two small fish. But Jesus wasn't looking for practical; He was looking for powerful.

Jesus told the disciples to have the crowd sit down in groups. Then He took the loaves and fish, blessed the food, and gave it to the disciples to distribute.

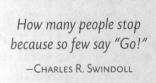

How many people stop because so few say "Go!"

—CHARLES R. SWINDOLL

Did Jesus need the disciples' help? No. But He chose to include them in the miracle. He wanted them to see that He believed in them.

Now, let's fast-forward in Jesus' ministry and His relationship with His disciples. He shared with them the potential He saw in them. Like a coach who believes in his team, Jesus rallied the 12 disciples: "Go rather to the lost sheep of Israel. As you go, preach this message: 'The kingdom of heaven is near.' Heal the sick, raise the dead, cleanse those who have leprosy, drive out demons. Freely you have received, freely give" (Matthew 10:6-8).

Before His ascension He gave them one last pep talk: "Go and make disciples of all nations, baptizing them in the name of the Father and of the Son and of the Holy Spirit, and teaching them to obey everything I have commanded you. And surely I am with you always, to the very end of the age" (Matthew 28:19-20). They had observed, learned, and practiced. Now it was time to step out into the world and participate in ministry without Jesus' physical presence. He believed in them, and He let them know it.

"I tell you the truth," Jesus said, "anyone who has faith in me will do what I have been doing. He will do even greater things than these, because I am going to the Father" (John 14:12). Oh, my. Did you notice? Jesus wasn't just talking about the 12 disciples. He was also talking about you! Jesus believes in you! He is the wind beneath our wings.

Expecting the Best

Both vultures and hummingbirds are winged creatures. Vultures have a knack for finding dead and decaying animals because that is what they are looking for. Hummingbirds have a knack for spotting nectar in beautiful flowers because that is what they are looking for. Our words are a reflection of what we are looking for in people, circumstances, and life.

I heard a story of a traveler nearing a great city. He stopped and asked a woman seated by the wayside, "What are the people like in the city?"

"How were the people where you came from?"

"A terrible lot," the traveler responded. "Mean, untrustworthy, detestable in all respects."

"Ah," said the woman. "You will find them the same in the city ahead."

Scarcely was the first traveler gone when another one stopped and also inquired about the people in the city before him. Again the old woman asked about the people in the place the traveler had left.

"They were fine people; honest, industrious, and generous to a fault. I was sorry to leave," declared the second traveler.

Responded the wise woman: "So you will find them in the city ahead."

The wise old woman understood that we tend to see people through a lens of our own making. Whatever we are looking for is generally what we will find. Some people have a gift for bringing out the best in people.

Gayle experienced both the vultures and the hummingbirds in her own life. In the first grade she and her best friend, Jen, were reprimanded for talking in class. "If you two don't stop talking," the teacher scolded, "I'm going to tape your mouths shut!"

Later Jen whispered something to Gayle. "Shh," Gayle mouthed, not wanting to get in trouble.

The teacher never saw Jen speak, but she did see Gayle's lips move. Out came the tape. "I can still see her grinning behind those cat-glasses," Gayle recalled. "She didn't put tape over Jen's mouth, just mine. I was humiliated, and thus began my years of quiet shyness. I withdrew and felt marred for many years to come."

A similar experience occurred in the third grade when Gayle was sent to the principal's office for correcting a teacher's spelling mistake on the chalkboard. Her insecurity was also compounded by words from her careless father. "You are so stupid!" he'd say. "Why are you so dumb?" "You'll never amount to anything!"

"I believed my dad," Gayle confided. "I thought I was a failure at everything. By the time I entered junior high, I was sad, lonely, afraid to trust people, and afraid to make new friends. I believed I was stupid and no good."

But something happened to turn Gayle's life around. She went off to college and lived with an amazing couple who pumped courage into her damaged soul. Carole and Emmett overflowed with positive and encouraging words for Gayle and showered her with love and kindness.

"I found myself dazed over the fact that people could be so kind, welcoming, and lovable toward me," Gayle remembered. "Oftentimes I found myself wondering how one woman could have so many positive encouraging words! Not once did Carole direct a negative word toward me. She believed in me and my abilities. Her positive words and actions stirred in me a desire to thrive in all areas of my life. I had always felt stupid, but with her encouragement as the wind beneath my wings, I soared to the top of my class. I realized I was not stupid after all. Like the scarecrow from *The Wizard of Oz*, I had a brain, but had never realized it until this wonderful woman pointed it out. It is amazing how profoundly the encouraging words of just one woman so drastically changed the life of a pitiful, broken teenager who showed up in her driveway one beautiful fall day so many years ago. Her words transformed me into a confident woman with a heart for God."

Reigniting the Fire

Jesus peered into Peter's eyes and saw the anguish of His friend's failure. Several hours earlier, Jesus had warned Peter that Satan desired to sift him like wheat (Luke 22:31). Jesus predicted that Peter would deny Him three times before the cock crowed the next morning, but Peter vehemently refused to believe he would ever deny his Lord. "I will lay down my life for you!" Peter cried. Now, just a few hours later, as the rooster announced the dawn of a new day, Peter despaired at his own weakness. The 12 disciples who had once flamed like 12 stoked cinders now smoldered like separated briquettes.

Would Jesus allow their spark to go out? Or would He gather the men and stoke the fire of passion once again? I am so thankful Jesus chose to stoke the fire. I am so thankful He sees our potential among the ruins and chooses to reignite our flame when the harsh winds of life try to extinguish our fire or the pressures of this world seem to snuff out our dreams.

After Jesus' resurrection, He appeared on a beach where He had built a fire. Peter and several other disciples joined their risen Savior for a meal of roasted fish and encouragement. (Read the whole story in John 21.)

Jesus said to Simon Peter: "Simon son of John, do you truly love me more than these?"

"Yes, Lord," he said, "you know that I love you."

Jesus said, "Feed my lambs."

Again Jesus said, "Simon son of John, do you truly love me?"

He answered, "Yes, Lord, you know that I love you."

Jesus said, "Take care of my sheep."

The third time he said to him, "Simon son of John, do you love me?"

Peter was hurt because Jesus asked him the third time, "Do you love me?" He said, "Lord, you know all things; you know that I love you."

Jesus said, "Feed my sheep."

Peter's fire had been snuffed out by his weak words, but Jesus stoked the embers of his heart with wonderful words that said, "I believe in you, Peter." We can do the same.

Once there was a young African-American girl with great singing potential. However, she made her debut at New York's Town Hall too early. She wasn't ready, and the critics destroyed her. She returned home to Philadelphia in disgrace. Her church had pooled their meager dimes and nickels for "The Fund for Marian Anderson's Future," and after her apparent failure, she didn't know how she would ever face them again.

> *A person may not be as good as you tell her she is, but she'll try harder thereafter.*
>
> —Author Unknown

For more than a year, Marian was held captive by depression and disgrace. But while her hopes smoldered near extinction, her mother would not allow the dream to die. She continued to use her words to keep the dream alive. "You have a gift," she said. "This failure is only temporary."

Finally, her mother's words began to sink in. "Marian, grace must come before greatness," she said. "Why don't you think about this failure a little and pray about it a lot?"

Marian Anderson, who did go on to become a great vocalist who helped others reach their dreams, said, "Whatever is in my voice, faith put there. Faith and my mother's words: 'Grace must come before greatness.'"[2]

That is the potential of a woman's words. Just as Jesus used His words to encourage hopes and reignite extinguished dreams, we can use our words to fan sparks of potential into a blazing flame.

Open Doors

Little Carolyn loved to paint, and when her art teacher asked the class to paint a horse, she painted a picture of a pink-and-purple polka-dotted pony. But rather than praise Carolyn's creativity, she rebuked her for "painting a lie." "There is no such thing as a pink-and-purple polka-dotted pony," she replied. "No talent here."

So Carolyn decided that no one would ever see her painting again. She only painted the walls in her closet, a place where no one would see. However, one day her mother took some friends up to Carolyn's closet to see a dress she had made for her. When they opened the door, the ladies were surprised to see the walls covered in beautiful art.

"Why, Carolyn," her mother exclaimed. "You're a painter!"

Today, Carolyn Blish is an award-winning member of the American Watercolor Society and Allied Artists of America. Reproductions of her paintings are in fine art galleries, and her prints have received international acclaim.[3]

Is there someone in your world who has talent hidden away in a closet? Perhaps you hold the key to opening the door and setting them on a path to success.

Once there was a little boy who was trying out for his school play. His mother busied herself in the kitchen as her son waited by the phone for a call from the teacher to announce his part. Finally, the phone rang and little Billy ran to pick up the receiver. In just a few moments, he dashed back to his mother with excitement and pride. "Guess what," he exclaimed. "I've been chosen to clap and cheer!"[4]

Do you see the wisdom of this teacher? Her words could have discouraged a child who had hoped to have a leading part in the play.

But she crafted her words in such a way that she ended up fueling his excitement rather than snuffing it out. We also can use our words to benefit others, even in the framework of apparent failure.

Giving Hope to the Hopeless

Jon Robinson was a longtime media personality in Charlotte, North Carolina, but when he was passed over for an anchor position he thought he had earned, he quit his job at the local television network and sank into a depression. He was hurting and alone. But an unusual twist of fate turned his life around. It all began with a wrong number.

Jon was sitting in the Waterfront Park in Charleston, South Carolina, watching seagulls soaring happily over the pristine harbor. He had taken a job in Charleston, but he missed his son back in Charlotte and mourned that he only got to see him on weekends. He was mulling over his sorrows, pondering the twists and turns of his life and wondering what his next step should be. Jon wasn't happy with his circumstances and knew he was drinking too much. Something needed to change.

Jon's musings were interrupted by the familiar ring of his cell phone.

He never answered his cell phone unless he knew the caller. He didn't recognize the number, but for some reason he mechanically answered and said, "Hello?"

"I'm sorry," the caller apologized. "I must have the wrong number."

"No problem," Jon replied.

"Well, before I hang up, I want you to know that God loves you and I'm praying for you," the caller continued.

"You must be out of your mind."

"No. This is a message God wants you to hear."

Jon was intrigued by this woman and they began talking. Before he knew it, he was pouring out his heart and sharing his personal and professional problems. As he told of his hurt, she shared her

> *Words—so innocent and power-less as they are, as standing in a dictionary, how potent for good and evil they become, in the hands of one who knows how to combine them!*
>
> —NATHANIEL HAWTHORNE

hope. He poured out his misery; she poured in her ministry. The caller told Jon about the hope and healing of Jesus Christ, and God began to open his eyes to the possibility of a new life.

For most of his life, Jon had been an agnostic. But since that "wrong number" with the "right answer," Jon has committed his life to Jesus Christ. "I am a Christian. I've had an awakening."[5] That is the power of a woman's words. While we blunder through our days with wrong turns and wrong numbers, we have the right answer! We possess the potential to change the course of a life for all eternity.

Restoring the Dream

I live in Charlotte, North Carolina, 200 miles from the coast. And yet our local Wal-Mart has a random smattering of seagulls that soar overhead and eat French fries and other debris from neighboring fast food restaurants. The truth is, the seagulls are lost. They've taken a wrong turn. And instead of discovering where they went wrong, they've settled for an asphalt parking lot rather than the salty sea. They've reconciled themselves to feeding on the refuse and trash of harried shoppers rather than the fresh seafood cuisine of their feathered forefathers.

It's not just the seagulls who are lost...who have forgotten the reason for their very existence, the habitat for which they were created to survive and thrive. Human beings have done the same. Many have become lost. They are standing in the parking lot of life subsisting off the refuse of fast living.

Someone needs to point them to the ocean of opportunity, the sea of success, the shore of satisfaction. And I'm not taking about money or materialism...those things *are* mere French fries compared to the abundant life God has for His image bearers. "'I know the plans I have for you,' declares the LORD, 'plans to prosper you and not to harm you, plans to give you hope and a future'" (Jeremiah 29:11).

Hang the fire extinguisher back in the corner and become an encourager who fans even the smallest spark of potential into flame. Let's send those "gulls" and "buoys" back to the sea of opportunity where they belong.

Now let's turn our attention to five areas of our lives where we can have a great impact with our words and one that can have a great impact on us.

The *People* We Impact

*T*HE *P*OWER OF A *W*OMAN'S *W*ORDS TO *H*ER *C*HILDREN

Love your children with all your heart...Praise them for important things...Praise them a lot. They live on it like bread and butter.

—LAVINA CHRISTENSEN FUGAL, 1995 MOTHER OF THE YEAR

WHY DO WE START WITH CHILDREN? Because that's where God starts with us. We come into the world as malleable souls who are shaped and molded by the people in our own little world. And before you know it, we are sitting at the potter's wheel surrounded by little people of our own.

I have often heard that it is better to build children than repair adults, so let's start our journey of discovering the power of a woman's words and the people we impact with those who are most vulnerable...children.

From the time a child emerges from the safety of a mother's womb, he or she is shaped and molded by the power of a mother's words. With her eyes locked on her new little bundle of squirming love, she coos, comforts, and coaxes this miraculous gift from God and becomes the mirror in which the child sees himself.

A mother cheers for her bundle of joy when he rolls over, laughs, and kicks his tiny feet into the air. She even gives a hurrah when her precious angel burps! A mother encourages her babe when he shakes a rattle, holds a cup, points to a color, and responds to his name. But most of all, she lets her child know "I love you just because you're mine."

It is an awesome responsibility, this job called motherhood. We have the privilege of shaping and molding an eternal soul for a very short, very fleeting moment of time. And one of the primary ways we accomplish this feat is with the words we speak.

When we hold that tiny bundle in our arms for the very first time, a flood of hopes and dreams emerges like a great blue whale cresting to spout his spray into the air. But somewhere in the day-to-day busyness of life, encouraging words can get lost among the to-dos and not-to-dos. We need to take a fresh look at motherhood and recapture the commitment to be the great encouragers along a child's journey toward adulthood.

Whether you have children of your own or have the privilege of other people's children in your life, you have the ability to shape a child's heart for good or bad. Marion observed the power of *her* mother's words in the life of a little girl who seemed to have lost her way.

Mama's Plan

The year was 1942 and Marion was entering first grade. She loved everything about school: the smell of the chalk and color of the crayons; the way the old wooden floors smelled after Jim, the janitor, had waxed them; having her own desk that was just her size; and her teacher, Miss Edna. She decided that all angels must have blue eyes and smell like Jergen's lotion because that was what Miss Edna looked and smelled like. The only thing she did not like about first grade was Mildred.

Now, Mildred had already been to first grade one time and she was bigger than everybody else. She didn't have any friends and seemed to concentrate on making enemies. Because Marion was one of the smallest in the class, Mildred singled her out as her number one enemy. Each day, as Marion walked home from school, Mildred would taunt her. She would come up behind her and step on the backs of her shoes, causing them to slide down. Then when Marion stopped to adjust them, Mildred would slap her hard on the back. Marion dreaded the walk home.

Each day, when the school bell rang for dismissal, Marion blinked back the tears that threatened to spill from her fearful eyes. Eventually, Marion's mother figured out something was wrong at school. Marion reluctantly told her mom about Mildred but begged her not to intervene, knowing it would only make it worse.

"You can't do anything, Mama," Marion cried. "You can't. Everyone will think I'm a baby."

Marion's father had died a few years earlier and her mother worked very hard. It was impossible for her to drive or walk Marion to school, and she didn't have any brothers or sisters to look after her. The problem seemed looming and a solution impossible.

The following day, Miss Edna asked Marion to stay after school to clean the erasers. Thinking that perhaps Mildred would be long gone by the time she walked home, Marion's heart leapt with joy (and appreciation). However, when Marion left school, her tormentor was waiting at the top of the hill.

Seeing her daughter in tears once more, this wise mother came up with a plan. The following day she decided to walk her daughter to school. Marion was skeptical, to say the least.

"Why couldn't my mother understand that no plan she had dreamed up was going to work?" Marion later recounted. "We bundled up against the bitter cold and started walking up the hill. Maybe we wouldn't see Mildred, I hoped. But my mother had this confident look. I knew the look well, and I had a sinking feeling that we would see Mildred and that Mother would use her 'plan.'

"Sure enough, just as we got to the top of the hill and had to go in one direction to school and my mother in the opposite direction to her job at the bank, we spotted Mildred. We waited a few horrible moments as Mildred approached us. She pretended not to see us when she realized I had my mother with me.

"'Hello, Mildred,' Mother said quietly. Mildred stopped, frozen as still as a statue. Her hands and face were bright red from the intense cold. Her oversized coat hung open. There were only two buttons on it. The rest were missing. Underneath she wore a cotton dress, as though it were summer. I was wrapped up so snugly, I could hardly walk. I even had to wear undershirts.

> There are many ways to measure success; not the least of which is the way your child describes you when talking to a friend.
>
> —AUTHOR UNKNOWN

"Mother stooped down to Mildred's level. She didn't say anything at first. Instead she rapidly buttoned Mildred's coat and turned up the collar around her neck. Then she fastened back this stubborn piece of hair that forever hung in Mildred's face. I stood off to one side watching our breath linger in front of our faces in the frigid morning air, praying that no students would happen by and that my mother's plan would be over quickly.

"'I'm Marion's mother. I need your help, Mildred.'

"Mildred looked intently at my mother with an expression I couldn't identify. Their faces were inches apart.

"My mother's gloved hands held Mildred's cold ones as she spoke. 'Marion doesn't have any brothers or sisters. She sort of needs a special best friend at school. Someone to walk up the hill with her after school. You look like you'd be a fine friend for her. Would you be Marion's friend, Mildred?'

"Mildred chewed on her bottom lip, blinking all the time, and then nodded.

"'Oh, thank you!' Mama said with certain confidence and gratitude. 'I just know you are someone I can depend on.' Then she hugged

Mildred long and hard. She gave me a quick hug and called to us as though nothing unusual had happened. 'Bye, girls. Have a good day.'"

Both girls continued walking to school, stiffly, like mechanical dolls staring straight ahead. Once Marion cut her eyes over toward Mildred and saw something she had never seen before...Mildred was smiling.

Time passed and Marion and Mildred became best friends. As a matter of fact, Mildred starting having lots of friends. She started making good grades, and her desk wasn't so messy anymore. And she always wore her coat collar flipped up and that scraggly piece of hair pinned over to the side, just the way Marion's mom had fixed it. On Valentine's Day, when all the kids cut out cards from red, pink, and white construction paper, Mildred gave Marion a store-bought card and signed it *From Your Best Friend, Mil.*[1]

What was Mama's plan? Her plan was to give encouraging words to a little girl who had been knocked down by life. To tell a floundering child that someone believed in her, trusted her, and entrusted her with her most prized possession. Those words changed the course of Mildred's life.

Verbal Homework

Studies show that in the average home, ten negative comments are made for every positive one. Also, it takes four positive comments to counteract one negative comment.[2] With that ratio, it's easy to understand why so many children are discouraged and suffer from a poor self-image.

We can't always see the destructive potential of our words, but let's imagine the following scenario. Your child gets up in the morning and dresses in a shingled outfit much like the Jolly Green Giant on the vegetable commercials. The only difference is the outfit is made of Post-it Notes. Every time you question his worth, criticize, make him feel guilty, incapable, insufficient, or unattractive, the hurtful words are scribbled across a slip of yellow paper and it flutters to the ground. Perhaps when you see the paper begin to fall, you realize the effect of your hurtful words and try to stick the paper back on with a positive word. However, it won't stick. The child goes off to school and hears more discouraging words and more shingles fall to the ground. Finally, at the end of the day, the child comes home, exposed, naked, and insecure—and rightly so.

As a mom, we can cover our kids with positive words so that when the negative ones cause a Post-it Note to fall, they won't even know it's missing. But it takes a lot of work.

> *Affirming words from moms and dads are like light switches. Speak a word of affirmation at the right moment in a child's life, and it's like lighting up a whole roomful of possibilities.*
>
> —Gary Smalley and John Trent

Paul wrote to the Colossians, "Fathers, do not provoke or irritate or fret your children [do not be hard on them or harass them], lest they become discouraged and sullen and morose and feel inferior and frustrated. [Do not break their spirit]" (Colossians 3:21 AMP). Can I add something to Paul's exhortation? Mothers, don't you do it, either.

It's a terrible thing to be a part of a family when the only things that are noticed are mistakes. The pain from constant criticism and correction can become a chronic source of insecurity long after the child has become an adult. It is our job, our "homework," to instruct our children, but when we are continually pointing out their faults and failures, they tend to simply stop trying.

We must always remember that children are children and they will act like children. Children are not miniature adults. I remember when my husband was in dental school at the ripe old age of 23. It was his first time treating a four-year-old little girl, and he was unprepared for the crocodile tears that escaped her eyes.

"You'll be fine," Steve assured her. "You be a big girl now."

Then she looked up at him with big blue eyes that melted his heart. "But I'm not a big girl," she said. "I'm just a little girl."

That's what we must always remember. No matter how frustrated or angry we become…kids are kids and they will act like kids.

Here's an idea. Try catching a child doing something right and then praise him or her for it! "Mary, I saw the way you helped your brother with his homework! Great job." "Brian, I noticed how well you cleaned the mud off of your shoes before you came in the house. Thank you." Consider the words to this poem:

Tale of Two Households

"I got two A's," the small boy said.
His voice was filled with glee.
His father very bluntly asked,
"Why didn't you get three?"

"Mom, I've got the dishes done,"
The girl called from the door.
Her mother very calmly said,
"Did you sweep the floor?"

"I mowed the grass," the tall boy said,
"And put the mower away."
His father asked him with a shrug,
"Did you clean off the clay?"

The children in the house next door
Seemed happy and content.
The same things happened over there,
But this is how it went.

"I got two A's," the small boy said.
His voice was filled with glee.
His father proudly said, "That's great;
I'm glad you belong to me."

"Mom, I got the dishes done,"
The girl called from the door.
Her mother smiled and softly said,
"Each day I love you more."

"I've mowed the grass," the tall boy said.
"And put the mower away."
His father answered with much joy,
"You've made my happy day!"

Children deserve just simple praise
For the tasks they're asked to do.
If they're to lead a happy life,
So much depends on you!

AUTHOR UNKNOWN

I remember taking my son, Steven, to an amusement park just before he began fourth grade. It was hot, the lines were long, and I began to feel queasy from being gyrated and jerked to sudden stops from 60 miles per hour. Feeling quite the martyr, I was just about to remind Steven how lucky he was to have a mother like me to bring him to a place like this. But before the words escaped from my mouth, the Holy Spirit gently stopped me. Was that what I really wanted to say? Would those words make Steven feel "lucky" or would they make him feel guilty, as though he owed me something?

Instead of uttering my initial thought, I wrapped my arms around my precious young son and said, "Steven, I am so lucky to have a son like you that I can bring to a place like this!" With those words, a dimpled smile spread across his precious face, and I was thankful for the splash of the watery roller coaster that disguised the tears streaming down my face.

If I had spoken that first sentence, Steven would not have felt lucky to have a mom like me at all. He would have felt guilty and that he needed to pay me back for my "kindness." However, the revised version made him feel special, treasured, and loved.

Now, who was encouraged? Actually, we both were.

Perhaps you have some old tapes from your past that you tend to replay with your children. Did your mother make comments that caused you to feel guilty or as if you were indebted to her for the care she gave you? Perhaps she still does. Many moms could be travel agents for guilt trips. Is that how you want to be remembered?

Guilt is like verbal heartburn or acid reflux of the soul. It just keeps on coming back and coming back. But, Mom, we can change the verbal menu and decide not to serve up a dish of words that cause indigestion!

I had success with my words that day at the amusement park, but not every day has been a banner day. I have used my words to tear down instead of build up. I have failed many times. "The tongue is a fire, the very world of iniquity," as James so aptly points out (James 3:6 NASB). It can only be tamed by the power of the Holy Spirit. God has given those who are in Christ Jesus, the power of the Holy Spirit. He is referred to as our "Helper." Just like a wild lion who is trained by hours and hours of discipline, so our tongue can be tamed by spending time with God and through practice. We will get into how to tame this wild beast more in a later chapter.

Lingering Echoes

Our words do more than just make our children feel good. Our words can make them feel like somebody who can accomplish great dreams or like a nobody who is destined to be a loser. As children, we learn many cute little sayings. "Early to bed, early to rise, makes a man healthy, wealthy, and wise." "Don't put all your eggs in one basket." "A stitch in time saves nine." But one adage I remember reciting as I was mercilessly teased by the neighborhood boys: "Sticks and stones may break my bones, but words will never hurt me." Nothing could be further from the truth, for the pain of a hurtful word lingers long after the pain of a broken bone is forgotten. And when a mother utters the hurtful words, the effects can linger for a lifetime.

Bob told me about how his mother's hurtful words had lingered for many years. When he was in his twenties, he worked in a family business with his father. He was very diligent and won recognition as the "Young Businessman of the Year." He, his young bride, and his parents traveled to Washington, DC, where he would accept his award. He sat eagerly at the dinner table, anticipating hearing his name announced from the podium. Then his mother leaned over and said, "You need to thank your father for this, Bob. You didn't really earn this award. Your father earned it for you."

Twenty years had passed when Bob told me this story, but the pain etched on his face was as though it had happened the day before. "Words will never hurt me?" Nothing could be further from the truth.

Ruthie had the same hollowness in her heart. All her life she longed to hear her mother say, "Ruthie, you are so beautiful!" While she never heard them as a child, it was her wedding day when she thought her dream would come true. However, as her mother straightened her veil and posed with her daughter dressed in a magnificent beaded wedding gown, the words were never spoken. As if someone forgot to light the candles on the cake, Ruthie passed the day without the words her little-girl heart longed to hear.

Oh, friend, we should never be stingy when it comes to speaking good words to children, but rather sow them profusely. Scatter compliments! Plant affirmation! Sow courage! Water with kindness! Fertilize with prayer! There will be plenty of other people along life's journey who will sow weeds of doubt, dread, and discouragement. We have the power to wash those seeds away before they have a chance to take root or pull the weeds before they choke out the tender shoots.

Chief Cheerleader or Chief Critic

Every day we have a choice. Will we build up our children or tear them down? Will we speak words of life or of death? Are we a child's chief cheerleader or chief critic? William Barclay tells a story of a mom who made a choice to speak words of life. One day Benjamin West's mother went out, leaving him in charge of his little sister, Sally. In his mother's absence, he discovered some bottles of colored ink, and to amuse Sally, he began to paint her portrait. In doing so, he made quite a mess of things…spilling numerous ink splotches here and there. When his mother returned, she saw the mess but said nothing about it. Instead, she deliberately looked beyond all that as she picked up the piece of paper. Smiling, she exclaimed, "Why, it's Sally!" She then stooped and kissed her son. From that time on, Benjamin West would say, "My mother's kiss made me a painter."[3]

My son ran cross-country in high school. On the way to one of Steven's races, I got lost. The races only last about 20 minutes, so it is pretty important to be on time. Well, I arrived just as the runners were walking off the trail, missing the race altogether.

On the way home, Steven said, "You know, there were so many parents and fans cheering for the other teams and hardly anybody yelling for us. When I ran by and heard them cheering for everyone else, it actually made me go slower. I didn't think it would really matter that much, but it did."

Dr. Donald Clifton of SRI/Gallup Poll conducted a study to see if there was a correlation between an athlete's performance and the presence of family members in the audience. The evidence showed that those athletes who had moms and other family members watching from the sidelines were more likely to perform at a higher level than those who had no one cheering them on.[4]

If we leave our child's cheering section—if our seat is vacant—the child will look for someone else to fill it. That someone is usually a peer. Then the child begins to try to please whoever is occupying that seat in the stands. So dust off those pom-poms! Ready that megaphone! Be about the business of becoming your child's greatest fan!

Author Karol Ladd gives this analogy:

Consider the analogy of a luxury car and the fuel we put into it to make it run. The positive affirmation we give our children is the gasoline we put in the tank of their car. The car has value whether we put gas in the tank or not; but if we want the car to go somewhere and stay in good condition, we need to fill it up with quality fuel. Our kids have great value. The more we fill them with the fuel of encouragement, the more energy they will have to reach their goals and follow their dreams.[5]

A mother's support means a great deal to her child. She is an encourager whose voice can be heard echoing in the distance, pumping courage and confidence into her children's hearts. She's the cheerleader on the sidelines who knows that an uplifting word, offered at the right moment, might make the difference between her children finishing well or collapsing along the way.

Uniquely Created

Every child wants to know that he or she is unique and special—unlike any other child ever created. Most teens think they are different, but not in a good way. They see themselves as not as pretty, smart, athletic, popular, funny, and cool as other teens. Adolescents tend to see themselves through the critical lens of pop culture.

But just suppose a child has a mother who has explained about his or her uniqueness. Just suppose a child has a mother who reminds the child of God's distinctive design and plan for her life…that she possesses features and talents that were created in her for a unique, God-ordained purpose. I wonder if the words would serve as a defense for the insecurities that tend to slap the young adolescent around like harsh winds.

God puts gifts and talents in each child, and it's the parent's responsibility to discover the treasure hidden beneath the freckled face, tousled hair, and muddy feet. A wise mom looks beyond pink hair bows, pouty lips, and rosy cheeks. By being specific with our praise, a child believes what you perceive. Again, you become the mirror from which your child sees herself.

My friend Glynnis has five children. She is an expert at discovering the uniqueness of each child. She studies, observes, listens, and ponders these fascinating creatures, and then she helps them recognize their distinctive gifts. Here are her words of wisdom for us.

> Having three boys, who by nature are competitive, challenged me to be creative in how I encouraged their individual strengths. When they started comparing themselves to each other in athletics and academics, they began to focus on their own personal weaknesses. One thing we did to help them see their strengths was to compare each one to an animal that shared a similar characteristic. Josh is solid and strong, and he became our lion. Robbie is thin and nimble, and he became our cheetah. Dylan is fast and savvy and he was our jaguar. The boys loved being compared to a beautiful animal, and they caught a glimpse of their unique abilities.
>
> When I was a little girl, my dad used to count my freckles with pleasure. As a result, I grew up liking my freckles. To help my boys feel better about their physical features, I've always told them how much I enjoy very specific parts of their makeup. "I love your brown eyes," I'd say. "They remind me of chocolate, and you know how much I love chocolate!" "Dylan, I love your wavy hair," I'd muse. "It reminds me of the ocean." "Robbie, I love your straight hair," I'd remark. "It shines just like gold when the sun shines on it."
>
> Now that we have adopted two little girls from Africa, I am finding new challenges to help them see their uniqueness. The younger girl, Ruth, immediately started talking about how much she loved our white skin and how she wished she were white. "But look how the sun glistens on your beautiful brown skin when I put lotion on it," I said. Pretty soon her smile and attitude matched the glow of her beautiful brown skin. It has been months since she has mentioned her skin and she loves to put lotion on it.

Most of all, I have taught each of my kids to be the best at who God made them to be. "Joshua," I'd say, "be the best Joshua you can be." "Dylan, be the best Dylan you can be." "Robbie, be the best Robbie you can be." "Ruth, be the best Ruth you can be." "Cathrine, be the best Cathrine you can be." It is a joy to watch each one of my children blooming into the confident young men and women God wants them to be. Thankfully, they don't try to be anyone else.

Jeremiah 29:11 says, "'I know the plans I have for you,' declares the LORD, 'plans to prosper you and not to harm you, plans to give you hope and a future.'" God has specific plans for each human being. While a mother doesn't know what those specific plans are for her children, she can give them the tools of discovery, point them to the treasure map, and help them see the clues along the way.

A mother's words can be the breeze that fills the sails of a child's hopes and dreams to propel them to new horizons. However, we must be careful that the wind that fills their sails sends them in the direction God has planned and not off course to a route of our own making.

Fearfully and Wonderfully Made

Did you notice how specific Glynnis was in her praise? "Great job," "You're terrific," and "Way to go!" are all wonderful pats on the back. However, being specific with praise is more powerful and makes a greater impact. "I couldn't believe how far you hit that baseball. Man, you've got an incredible swing." "That cartwheel was amazing. Your legs stuck up straight in the air just like a professional gymnast." "I noticed the way you helped Mary with her homework. You have such a generous heart. I want to be more like you."

Do you see the difference? Being specific moves encouraging words from good to great.

A great mom will discover a child's gifts and talents and then use her words to fertilize that gift. She will help them realize the words of the psalmist, "I praise you because I am fearfully and wonderfully made" (Psalm 139:14). If a child becomes good at one thing, he or she will believe that success is achievable in other areas of life as well and won't be afraid to attempt them. We don't have to be a millionaire to let our children know they are rich. Encouraging words are free for the giving with bountiful results.

Thomas Edison, one of America's greatest inventors, had this to say about the positive influence of his mother's words on his own life:

> I did not have my mother long, but she cast over me an influence which has lasted all my life. The good effect of her early training I can never lose. If it had not been for her appreciation and her faith in me at a critical time in my experience, I should never likely have become an inventor. I was always a careless boy, and with a mother of different mental caliber, I should have turned out badly. But her firmness, her sweetness, her goodness were potent powers to keep me on the right path. My mother was the making of me.[6]

While we do want to discover the uniqueness of each child, our praise must consist of verbal applause for more than appearance and talents. The most important traits we praise are those that exhibit godly character. The Bible calls these "fruit of the Spirit": love, joy, peace, patience, kindness, goodness, faithfulness, gentleness, and self-control (Galatians 5:22-23). If even a sprout of these fruits peeks through the soil, a wise mother will fertilize the sprout with positive words in hopes of a bountiful harvest.

Believing the Best

By the fifth grade, Howard Hendricks was bearing all the fruit of a kid who felt insecure, unloved, and angry at life. In other words, he was tearing the place apart. However, his teacher Miss Simon apparently thought he was blind to this problem because she regularly reminded him, "Howard, you are the worst behaved child in this school!"

So tell me something I don't already know! he thought to himself as he proceeded to live up (or down) to her opinion of him. I'll let Dr. Hendricks tell you the rest of the story.

> Needless to say, the fifth grade was probably the worst year of my life. Finally I graduated—for obvious reasons. But I left with Miss Simon's words ringing in my ears: "Howard, you are the worst-behaved child in this school!"
>
> You can imagine what my expectations were upon entering the sixth grade. The first day of class, my teacher Miss Noe went down the roll call, and it wasn't long before she came to my name. "Howard Hendricks," she called out, glancing from her list to where I was sitting with my arms folded, just waiting to go into action. She looked me over for a moment and then said, "I've heard a lot about you." Then she smiled and added, "But I don't believe a word of it!"
>
> I tell you, that moment was a fundamental turning point, not only in my education, but in my life. Suddenly, unexpectedly, someone believed in me. For the first time in my life, someone saw potential in me. Miss Noe put me on special assignments. She gave me little jobs to do. She invited me to come in after school to work on my reading and arithmetic. She challenged me with higher standards.
>
> I had a hard time letting her down…
>
> What made the difference between fifth grade and sixth? The fact that someone was willing to give me a chance. Someone was willing to believe in me while challenging me with higher expectations.[7]

Many times a child doesn't act capable because he is treated as though he is not. Goethe said, "Treat a man as he appears to be, and you make him worse. But treat a man as if he already were what he potentially could be, and you make him what he should be." Howard Hendricks experienced the power of a woman's words to change the course of his life. Today, he is a world renowned Bible teacher and theologian.

Lady Liberty

Each day hundreds of people ferry across the New York harbor to view the Statue of Liberty, who has welcomed weary travelers to the American shore. Lady Liberty was a gift of friendship from the people of France in 1886 and has stood as a symbol of freedom for thousands who have escaped the tyranny and poverty of distant lands. With torch held high, she proclaims, "Give me your tired, your poor, your huddled masses yearning to breathe free."

And who did the famous sculptor use as his inspiration for this beacon of freedom and faith? His mother. Frederic Bartholdi chose his own mother as the model for the Statue of Liberty to represent freedom and faith to all who enter the United States via the New York Harbor. Like a stately lighthouse that guides seafaring ships safely to shore, mothers stand as sentinels on the rough shoreline of life to guide their tiny fleet safely home and back out to sea.

When our children grow to maturity, whom will they think of when they reflect on their own heritage of freedom and faith? Oh, dear friend, I hope they, like Frederic Bartholdi, think of their moms, who held high the light of Jesus Christ and gave them roots to stand firm and wings to soar.

Fun Ideas to Encourage a Child

- Put notes in a lunchbox.
- Write a note on the bathroom mirror with soap.
- Put a note on a pillow.
- Tie a note around a favorite stuffed animal.
- Tuck a note in a textbook.

- Send an e-mail.
- Write a letter and actually send it through the mail.
- Send a card.
- Celebrate with a "You Are Special" plate.
- Make a list of 25 reasons you're glad she's your kid.
- Write Scripture prayers for him.
- Point out biblical character traits you see in her.

POWER-PACKED WORDS

Words to Avoid

- You should…
- You ought…
- You can't do anything right.
- You are driving me crazy!
- You make me so upset!
- You make me so angry!
- Why did you do that?
- Why can't you make good grades like your sister/ brother?
- Why can't you be sweet like your sister/brother?
- You are a liar. (Change to "You told a lie.")
- You are a thief. (Change to "You stole something.")
- Look at all I've done for you.
- You don't love me.
- You don't appreciate me.
- I've told you a thousand times.
- You'll never learn, will you?

Simply put: Avoid sarcasm, teasing, and subtle put-downs and jokes at a child's expense. If you have to add "I was just kidding" to any statement made to a child, it will most likely leave a wound.

Words Children Long to Hear

- Great job!
- I'm glad you're my son/daughter.
- I love spending time with you.
- I'll never forget the day you were born. You were such an incredible gift from God…and you still are.
- I like you!
- That was really great!
- I love the way you fixed your hair!
- That shirt looks great on you!
- You played that song beautifully!
- You are a great friend!
- You'll make a wonderful wife/husband some day!
- Thanks for cleaning your room. You did a great job.
- You teach me so much about life.
- You're so strong!
- I can always count on you.
- I trust you.
- You are God's special gift to me.
- You light up my day.
- My favorite part of the day is picking you up from school.
- I missed having you around today.
- You're such a good helper.
- I'm proud of you!

- Way to go!
- I knew you could do it!
- God made a masterpiece when He made you.
- You are such a treasure!
- You are one of God's greatest gifts to me.
- I'm behind you.
- I'm praying for you.
- That was so responsible.
- You're a joy.
- How did you get so smart?
- That was so creative.
- Hurray for you!
- Thank you.

THE POWER OF A WOMAN'S WORDS TO HER HUSBAND

I like not only to be loved, but also to be told that I am loved.

—GEORGE ELIOT

FOR 13 YEARS our family was blessed with a golden retriever named Ginger. We gave her to our son, Steven, for Christmas when he was five years old, and she still holds the blue ribbon as the best present to date. I can still remember the look of surprise on Steven's cherubic face when the "stuffed" animal began to move. "It's a puppy!" he exclaimed. "It's not a toy!"

And while Ginger was officially Steven's dog, and I was unofficially her primary caretaker, it was my husband, Steve, who held a special place in her heart. From the very beginning, Ginger loved Steve the best.

Ginger lollygagged her days away by sleeping in the driveway or lounging by the back steps. However, when my husband's car entered the neighborhood and turned the corner onto our shady Stratfordshire Drive, Ginger's ears perked up and her eyes began to beam. Suddenly infused with a burst of anticipatory energy, she would jump to her feet and run in circles. "He's home! He's home!" she seemed to say.

When Steve pulled into the garage and opened his car door, Ginger whined, ran to greet him, and rested her head on his left leg while he cooed and rubbed her ears. Steve's homecoming was the highlight of her day.

No wonder dog is called "man's best friend." Ginger was loyal, didn't nag, and loved Steve no matter how much or how little attention he paid to her on any given day. She was very forgiving and almost immediately forgot any injustice, such as withholding our dinner when we ate in her presence or being left behind when we traveled on vacation. Often at the mere sight of Steve, Ginger rolled over on her back and beckoned him to rub her tummy. She always responded to his touch as though it were heaven on earth. What man wouldn't love such a response from "his girl"?

And yet, when God created Adam and placed him in the Garden, only to determine that "it is not good for the man to be alone" (Genesis 2:15), He did not create a dog to be his loyal companion. God created a woman to fill the void in his life. She was called an *ezer* in the Hebrew—the original language of the Old Testament. Most Bible translations render the word *ezer* as "helper," but the word is packed with so much more meaning than a mere helper. Author Carolyn Custis James reveals the following:

> *Ezer* appears twenty-one times in the Old Testament. Twice, in Genesis, it describes the woman (Genesis 2:18,20). But the majority of references (sixteen to be exact) refer to God, or Yahweh, as the helper of his people. The remaining three references appear in the books of the prophets, who use it to refer to military aid. If language means anything, the *ezer,* in every case, is not a flunky or junior assistant but a very *strong* helper.[1]

We would be remiss if we looked at the word *ezer* or "helper" in only domestic terms. Adam didn't need someone to cook for him, clean up after him, or care for him. That was not the problem. The void in Adam's life was that he did not have a companion to work with him, rule the earth with him, love with him, procreate with him, and after the fall—struggle with him. A dog might have been an easier adjustment for Adam, but God decided Adam needed someone with words.

"Then God said, 'Let us make man in our own image'...So God created man in his own image, in the image of God he created him; male and female He created them" (Genesis 1:26-27). All through the Bible we see the word "man" used to refer to "mankind." As in this rendering of the Hebrew word, "man" does not mean "male." Just as a puppy is the offspring of a dog, the word "man" means offspring of a "hu-man." I point this out because many of the verses that we will examine in this book will use the word "man," but they pertain to women as well.

I have yet to find the man, however exalted his station, who did not do better work and put forth greater effort under a spirit of approval than under a spirit of criticism.

—CHARLES SCHWAB

I saw a placard recently that read, "I always have the last word with my wife. It's 'Yes, dear.'" We chuckle—but it's not really funny, is it? Perhaps "Yes, dear" are the very words Adam said to Eve.

As an *ezer* or a strong helper, how will we use our words? Will we use them to fortify or flatten, defend or defeat, complete or compete? The choice begins in our minds, runs through our hearts, and responds with our lips. Let's look at a few biblical examples of the power of a woman's words on the men in their lives.

Words Can Break a Man

Samson was God's chosen man during a time when the judges ruled Israel. From birth, he was destined to liberate Israel from the taunting Philistines. While Samson was incredibly strong in body, he was very weak in character. Among his character flaws was a weakness for women. In his early years, he saw a Philistine woman, liked the Philistine woman, and decided he had to have her. Regardless of his parents' warnings, he married the young vixen, and she slowly but surely used her words to lead him astray.

It all began when Samson was talking to some of the fellows at the wedding party. "'Let me tell you a riddle,' Samson said to them. 'If you can give me the answer within the seven days of the feast, I will give you thirty linen garments and thirty sets of clothes. If you can't tell me the answer, you must give me thirty linen garments and thirty sets of clothes.'

"'Tell us your riddle,' they said. 'Let's hear it.'

"He replied, 'Out of the eater, something to eat; out of the strong, something sweet'" (Judges 14:12-14).

The men were perplexed at the riddle and were in fear of losing the shirts off their backs, so they convinced Samson's bride to coax the answer out of him. She whined. She cried. She manipulated. He weakened. He vacillated. He caved. Samson revealed the answer to the riddle to his new wife, and she in turn told her friends. The Philistines kept their shirts and Samson lost his. As Samson stormed away in a flurry of fury, his father handed the bride over to one of his attendants as a parting gift.

Twenty years later, the power of a woman's ill-spoken words had faded in Samson's memory, and he fell in love with yet another Philistine woman, Delilah. The Philistines saw Samson's infatuation with one of their own as a pathway to discovering the secret to his supernatural strength.

Each of the Philistine officials offered Delilah 1100 shekels of silver to uncover the secret to his supernatural strength. "See if you can lure him into showing you the secret of his great strength and how we can overpower him so we may tie him up and subdue him" (Judges 16:5). Three times she begged him to tell her the secret source of his strength, and three times he led her astray. But the fourth time she whined. She cried. She manipulated. He weakened. He vacillated. He caved.

Listen to her words and imagine the lure. " 'How can you say, "I love you," when you won't confide in me? This is the third time you have made a fool of me and haven't told me the secret of your great strength.' With such nagging she prodded him day after day until he was tired to death" (Judges 16:15-16).

Unfortunately, Samson told Delilah the secret of his strength. He couldn't take the nagging any longer.

An anxious heart weighs a man down, but a kind word cheers him up.

PROVERBS 12:25

" 'No razor has ever been used on my head,' he said, 'because I have been a Nazirite set apart to God since birth. If my head were shaved, my strength would leave me, and I would become as weak as any other man'" (Judges 16:17).

After Samson divulged the secret to his strength, Delilah lured him to put his head in her lap, cooed him to sleep, and called for the enemies to come and shave his head. Samson's strength seeped out with each swipe of the blade. He was bound, blinded, and spent the rest of his days in bondage...because he succumbed to the power of a woman's ill-spoken words.

Oh, the power of a woman's words on a man who loves her. This is not the only example of a woman in the Bible who used her words to bring harm to her husband. Michal spoke against her husband, King David, for dancing with reckless abandonment before the Lord. However, her words ricocheted and brought a curse on her own life...no more children. Sarai used her words to convince her husband, Abram, to sleep with her servant girl rather than wait on God's promise to provide an heir through her. Her words resulted in the birth of Ishmael and the resulting conflict between the Arab and Jewish nations that still rages today. Eve used her words to convince her husband, Adam, to eat the forbidden fruit. Her words resulted in sin, condemnation, and spiritual death to every man and woman born under the curse.

Now, lest you grow discouraged at all these examples of how women used their words in a destructive manner, let me give you a word of hope. Just as sin was ushered into the world through the words of Eve, salvation and hope was ushered into the world by the words of Mary. When the angel Gabriel came to the young teenage virgin and announced that she would conceive a child by the immaculate conception of the Holy Spirit, she replied, "Behold, the bondslave of the Lord; may it be done to me according to your word" (Luke 1:38 NASB). She embraced God's will for her life and used her words to glorify Him in one of the most beautiful songs of praise recorded in the Bible (see Luke 1:46-55).

Words Can Debilitate a Man

My friend Nancy, like Delilah, used her words to manipulate and debilitate her husband. However, she didn't see the damage it was doing until she heard her words coming from another source. Let's let Nancy tell the story in her own powerful words:

> My brother Dan said, "I'm going home! Your bickering is driving me nuts. Your constant fighting's more irritating than chewing on tinfoil!"
>
> I defended our behavior. "Hey, it's not like we disagree about *everything*. Ron and I agree on all the major issues. We hardly ever fight about 'big stuff,' like how to spend our money, how to raise Nick, or who's a better driver (me). It's just the little stuff that gets to us."
>
> He sighed and said, "Well, I'm sick of hearing you go to war over where to put the towel rack, which TV shows to watch, or who left the lights on. It's all dumb stuff. None of it will matter a year from now. Why did you have to criticize the way he mowed the lawn? I know it wasn't perfect, but couldn't you just let it go?"

"No," I replied. "We are having company tomorrow, and I want the yard to be perfect. So I told him to fix it. Big deal! We were married in the seventies, and Helen Reddy told me that I had to roar if I wanted to be heard, so I roar—and it works, because he re-mowed the lawn and I won."

Dan paused, shook his head, and said, "If you keep this up, you may win the arguments but lose your husband."

I smacked him on the arm and said, "Oh, stop being so melodramatic!"

The next evening Ron and I went out to dinner with some friends we hadn't seen in several years. We remembered Carl as being funny and outgoing, but he seemed rather sad and looked exhausted. His wife, Beth, did most of the talking. She told us about her fabulous accomplishments at work and then endlessly bragged about her brilliant, college-bound children.

She didn't mention her husband except to criticize him.

After we ordered our dinner, she said, "Carl, I saw you flirting with that waitress!" (He wasn't.)

"Caarrrlll," she whined a little while later, "can't you do anything right? You are holding your fork like a little kid!" (He was.)

When he mispronounced an item on the dessert menu, his wife said, "No wonder you flunked out of college. You can't read!" She laughed so hard she snorted, but she was the only one laughing.

Carl didn't respond. He just looked over at us with an empty face and a blank stare. Then he shrugged his sad shoulders and looked away.

The rest of the evening was even more oppressive as she continued to harangue and harass him about almost everything he said or did. I thought, I *wonder if this is how my brother feels when I criticize Ron.*

We said goodbye to Beth and Carl and left the restaurant in silence. When we got in the car, I spoke first. "Do I sound like her?"

Ron said, "You're not *that* bad."

I asked, "How bad am I?"

"Pretty bad," he half whispered.

The next morning, as I poured water into the coffeepot, I looked over at my "Famous Quotes for Wives" calendar. "The wise woman builds her house, but the foolish tears it down with her own hands." *Or with her own mouth,* I thought.

"A nagging wife annoys like a constant dripping." *How did I turn into such a nag?*

"Put a guard over my mouth." *Oh, Lord, show me how!*

As I carefully spooned the vanilla nut decaf into the pot, I remembered the day I forgot the filter. The coffee was bitter and full of undrinkable grounds. I had to throw it away.

Then it dawned on me. *The coffee, without filtering, is like my coarse and bitter speech.*

I said, "Oh, God, please install a filter between my brain and my mouth. Help me to choose my words carefully and speak in smooth and mellow tones. Thank You for teaching me the lesson of the coffee filter. I won't forget it."

An hour later Ron timidly asked, "What do you think about moving the couch over by the window? We'll be able to see the TV better."

My first thought was, *That's a dumb idea! The couch will fade if you put it in the sunlight, and besides, you already watch too much TV.*

But instead of my usual hasty reply, I let the coarse thoughts drip through my newly installed filter and smiled as I said, "That might be a good idea. Let's try it for a few days and see if we like it. I'll help you move it!"

He lifted his end of the sofa in stunned silence. Once we had it in place, he asked with concern, "Are you okay? Do you have a headache?"

I chuckled. "I'm great, honey. Never better. Can I get you a cup of coffee?"

Ron and I recently celebrated our twenty-seventh wedding anniversary, and I'm happy to report that my "filter" is still in place—although it occasionally springs a leak! I've also expanded the filter principal beyond my marriage, and I have found it amazingly useful when I speak to telemarketers, traffic cops, and teenagers.[2]

Words Can Make a Man

Billy Graham is one of the greatest evangelists of our time. His lifelong mission of giving hope through a relationship with Jesus Christ has reached more than two billion people around the world. What began in a one-room office in Minneapolis, Minnesota, in 1950, grew to become the Billy Graham Evangelistic Association and has taken the gospel to the farthest corners of the globe. And while Mr. Graham has been celebrated by presidents, the people, and the press for his passion to preach the gospel, he would be quick to say that it is his wife, Ruth, who deserves the praise.

"Ruth and I were called by God as a team," he said. "She urged me to go, saying 'God has given you the gift of an evangelist. I'll back you. I'll rear the children and you travel and preach.'...I'd come home and she had everything so organized and so calmed down that they all seemed to love me. But that was because she taught them to."[3]

Yes, it was Billy Graham's face the multitudes gazed upon and his booming fiery sermons that drew thousands to Christ, but it was Ruth, his wife, who gave him the courage and strength to disappear down their long driveway and leave home to do what God had called him to do.

"They [the children] were mighty good about him being gone so much because they knew why he was gone." Ruth remembered.[4] And how did they gain that deep understanding of why Daddy was gone? Because of the power of one woman's words to instill the passion of the gospel and the urgency of the message that their father preached.

"Without Ruth's partnership and encouragement over the years, my own work would have been impossible," Mr. Graham said.

On June 14, 2007, Ruth Bell Graham, this amazing woman of God who used her words to give strength and courage to a farm boy from Charlotte, North Carolina, went home to be with God. At her funeral Billy Graham stood up to thank God for this precious gift of Ruth. "My wife, Ruth, was the most incredible woman I have ever known," he said. "Whenever I was asked to name the finest Christian I ever met, I always replied, 'My wife, Ruth.' She was a spiritual giant whose unparalleled knowledge of the Bible and commitment to prayer were a challenge and inspiration to everyone who knew her."[5]

That is the power of a woman's words to make her man...to help him be all that God intended.

My dictionary defines "encouragement" as "the act of inspiring others with renewed courage, renewed spirit, or renewed hope." That beautifully describes the power of Ruth Graham toward her husband.

"Yes, love believes all things. It sticks up for seemingly impossible dreams, cheering as those dreams struggle forward and applauding when they finally come true."[6] Just as Delilah used her words to break her man, Ruth used her words to make her man.

Words Can Devastate a Man

Perhaps you are holding this book with a heavy heart because you know that the words that you speak to your husband have not been loving, kind, encouraging, or supportive. Perhaps you've forgotten the thrill of the early years when he walked into a room, the warmth of endearment when he called on the phone, the joy of becoming one when body and soul united. Perhaps you realize that your very words have built a wall between lovers rather than a bridge between friends. Is change possible? Absolutely!

If you've read my book *Becoming the Woman of His Dreams: Seven Qualities Every Man Longs For,* then you are familiar with the story of Don and Jona. Jona experienced a dramatic change in the way she spoke to her husband; however, it was almost too late.

> Don was 27 years old when Jona first met him on a fall church beach retreat. Immediately, she knew he was exactly what she had always dreamed of in a husband. Don had a strong faith in God, a good job, a college degree, drive, and dreams for the future. He was physically fit, witty, adventurous, sexy, and just plain gorgeous. On top of that, he was constantly surrounded by women at the retreat who were vying for his attention.
>
> Jona could hardly believe her good fortune when Don asked her out upon their return home. Don and Jona dated only three months before he asked her to marry him, and before the spring beach retreat, on March 30, 1985, they were husband and wife.
>
> Their first year of marriage was a blissful blur of candlelight dinners, spontaneous lovemaking, and endless conversation. The icing on the one-year anniversary cake was the purchase of their first home. By their second anniversary, Don quit his job to start his own business. Life was clicking along at a steady pace toward acquiring the American Dream. By their third anniversary, Jona had their first child and joined the ranks of "stay-at-home mom." But after 24 months of Don's new business venture, the couple faced a second mortgage, a dwindling bank account, and looming personal loans. Jona was forced to go back to work, and seeds of discontentment, disrespect, and disenchantment began to take root.
>
> "I was so mad at Don for the mistakes I felt he had made," Jona explained. "Deep down, I wanted him to be God and to fulfill all my needs. He made a poor God. When my mother died, I sank into a clinical depression. I spent most of my time at home in bed. And even though I had two children by this time, I withdrew from being a mom as well as being a wife. I then began to eat...and eat. I went from 140 pounds to 240 pounds.

"Don and I had the perfect engagement, a beautiful wedding, and a fantasy honeymoon. But when the obstacles came, I wasn't prepared. I thought, *This is not the way the story goes. What happened to the fairy tale?*

"Though Don changed jobs about every other year, he always provided for our needs. It just drove me crazy that he couldn't stay put.

"I remember one day Don said, 'Why are you eating and gaining all this weight?' I shot back, 'I'm doing this because I don't want you to touch me. Besides, I can lose the weight if I want to, but you'll always be a loser.' Little by little, word by word, angry look by angry look, rejection by rejection, I began the process of destroying my husband. Comments like 'You're so stupid,' 'Duh,' and 'Can't you do anything right?' were constantly spewing from my mouth. I was in pain and I wanted Don to be in pain too. One day I made a list of all of Don's faults. He found the list, but I didn't even care."

Jona always thought that because Don was a Christian, he would never leave her. However, there came a point where he couldn't take the emotional turmoil any longer. On May 6, 2001, Don left. Jona had single-handedly destroyed her marriage and her man. On January 31, 2003, the divorce was final.

"Shortly after Don left, I woke up to God's still, small voice," Jona explained. "He seemed to say, 'Is this what you wanted? Did you want a divorce? Do you want Don to marry another woman and have your children torn between spending time in two different households? Do you want to be alone?' 'Oh, God,' I cried, 'What have I done?'"

While Don and Jona were officially divorced, God was not finished with either of them. God took Jona to a place of repentance and began to soften, remold, and remake her heart. That's what God does. He doesn't try to cover up our flaws; He starts from scratch and makes us new. While the divorce was final, God was only just beginning to work on Jona's heart.

"God took me to a place of repentance," she explained. "For the first time, through a support group, I saw clearly what I had done to destroy my marriage. I had always blamed our problems on Don changing jobs so often, but the real problem was my lack of respect for the God-appointed leader of my home. I was the real problem, and Don simply couldn't take it anymore. I had rejected him with my words, my appearance, and my withdrawal of physical touch."

Whether or not God could salvage the marriage, Jona made a commitment that she would allow God to salvage her.

Jona's heart longed to be reunited to Don, but her ultimate goal was to become the woman God wanted her to be. She immersed herself in Bible study and prayer, and she began to take an interest in her appearance. Interestingly, as the pounds began to drop, so did the scales that had covered her eyes.

"I began to understand what God's Word said about the relationship between a husband and wife. I was not Don's Holy Spirit. I was not the leader of my home. God had called me to respect Don as the leader, to honor him as a child of God, and to love him with my all. One day when Don came to pick up the boys, I shared with him what I had been learning.

"I told Don that I knew we were divorced, but I was making a commitment to submit to him. I didn't when we were married, but I did from that time forward.

"'That's fine,' he told me. 'But you need to know I'm moving on with my life.'

"'You can move on,' I said, 'But I'm staying right here.'"

Jona continued to encourage Don and give him her BEST.

"BEST stands for bless, edify, share, and touch," she explained. "I began to touch him when he came by the house. I'd pat his back or give him a quick hug. When I knew he was coming, I'd put on a nice dress and fix my hair. I'd tell him I was proud of how he

> *Let the wife make the husband glad to come home, and let him make her sorry to see him leave.*
>
> —MARTIN LUTHER

was handling the boys and share with him what God was teaching me. Some people told him I was trying to trick him and that he should ignore me, but it wasn't a trick. God had changed my heart, and I was committed, no matter what happened between us in the future, to never go back to being that woman I had been before.

"Sharon, I hate to tell you this," she said, "but for the first time I prayed for Don. I had never prayed for him before, but now I pray for him all the time."

Jona lost a hundred pounds and gained a beautiful glowing countenance. It was amazing. More than the change in her physical appearance, the glow of Jesus Christ shone through her radiant face.

One day Don said, "Jona, you look soooo good."

"Don, I know I look better, but what I want you to see is my heart."

"I do see it, Jona," he said with tears in his eyes. "But, I'm moving on."

Jona knew that Don had met someone else, and while she never said a discouraging word about his new relationship, she continued to love Don and gave him her BEST. When her mind went to the other woman, God whispered, *You don't need to know the details. Leave that to me. You just love him.*

Don was confused at times and a bit leery of the change. "Why do you think I'm wonderful, all of a sudden?" he asked her.

"Because now I see you through God's eyes," she explained. "I see that you are a wonderful man."

Don fell in love with Jona all over again. No, it wasn't a trick—it was a miracle. God has given them a second chance. They were remarried on August 24, 2003. He is the God of second chances.

Dear friends, Jona had so graciously allowed me to tell you her story because she has decided that she will do anything to help even one woman not make the same mistakes she made. She cried and cried all through the recounting of the story and relived the pain for you. "God allowed me to go to a terrible place," Jona explained. "My prayer is that others will not have to go to that place before they wake up and realize what they are doing to their men."[7]

If you see a glimpse of yourself in Jona's story, please know that it is never too late to change! God brings life from death, and He can certainly give us the power to change the way we speak. Be encouraged, my friend. If you are willing to use your words as an instrument of beauty, He is more than able to supply the power to do so.

Words Can Motivate a Man

Susan attended a class on how to appreciate her husband. Part of the assignment for the following week was to tell her husband something she admired about him. Her husband was shorter than she, but quite handsome. In all their years together she had never put her admiration into words. It was a big step for her. She didn't quite know how to start, even though she loved her husband. That evening while he was reading the paper, she sat down next to him on the sofa and began stroking his arm. After a bit, she stopped at the bicep and squeezed. He unconsciously flexed his muscle, and she said, "Oh, I never knew you were so muscular!" He put down the paper, looked at her, and inquired, "What else?" He was so starved for admiration, he wanted to hear more.

How about your man? When was the last time you told him that you loved his smile or admired his talent? Can't remember? Well, today could be the day! That's your homework. Use your words to build up that man of yours.

Sophia used her words to elevate and motivate her husband. He came home very discouraged and defeated. He had just lost his job and dreaded telling his wife the bad news. However, after explaining his plight, he was met with an unexpected response.

"Now," she said triumphantly as she clapped her hands in delight, "you can write your book!"

"Yes," replied the man, with sagging confidence. "And what shall we live on while I am writing it?"

To his amazement, she opened a drawer and pulled out a substantial amount of money.

"Where on earth did you get that?" he exclaimed.

"I have always known you were a man of genius," she told him. "I knew that someday you would write a masterpiece. So every week, out of the money you gave me for housekeeping, I saved a little bit. Here is enough to last us for one whole year."

From her trust, confidence, and encouraging words came one of the greatest novels of American literature. That was the year Nathaniel Hawthorne wrote *The Scarlet Letter*.[8]

Words Can Captivate a Man

The book of Proverbs has much to say about wives and words:

- Like a gold ring in a pig's snout is a beautiful woman who shows no discretion (Proverbs 11:22).

- A quarrelsome wife is like a constant dripping (Proverbs 19:13).

- Better to live on a corner of the roof than share a house with a quarrelsome wife (Proverbs 21:9; worth repeating—Proverbs 25:24).

- Better to live in a desert than with a quarrelsome and ill-tempered wife (Proverbs 21:19).

- A quarrelsome wife is like a constant dripping on a rainy day; restraining her is like restraining the wind or grasping oil with the hand (Proverbs 27:15-16).

Well, that's enough of that!

The book of Proverbs begins with a father warning his son against the ways of wicked women and ends with a mother teaching her son the joys of acquiring a godly wife.

> A wife of noble character who can find? She is worth far more than rubies. Her husband has full confidence in her and lacks nothing of value. She brings him good, not harm, all the days of her life...Her husband is respected at the city gate, where he takes his seat among the elders of the land...Her children arise and call her blessed; her husband also, and he praises her; "Many women do noble things, but you surpass them all" (Proverbs 31:10-12,23,28-29).

Can't you just see it now? Your husband is sitting at his desk, lost in thought about how blessed he is to have you as his wife. He holds your framed picture in his hand and moisture begins to pool in his eyes. He is captivated. *All the riches in the world are not to be compared with the jewel I have in this woman. What did I ever do to deserve her? God has given me such a gift. All our married life, she has done nothing but love me, bring out the best in me, and look out for my best interest. All the guys at the office are envious of our relationship. I see the way their eyes soften when she comes by just to tell me hello, grabs my hand when we're at office functions, or pecks me on the cheek for no apparent reason. I notice that her loving words to me are in stark contrast to some of the cutting remarks of other wives...and so do my friends. I look around at the accomplishments of my life, but having this woman as my wife is my greatest. Sure, there are many women out there in the world who are accomplishing great feats, but my wife...well, she surpasses them all.*

What a picture! That's the woman I want to be. My words have the power to make it so.

POWER-PACKED WORDS

Twenty-Five Things Never to Say to Your Husband

- I told you so.
- You're always in a bad mood.
- You just don't think.
- It's all your fault.
- What's wrong with you?
- All you ever do is complain.
- I can't do anything to please you.
- You made your bed; now lie in it.
- You should have thought about that before.
- You never listen to me.
- All you care about is yourself.
- I don't know why I put up with you.
- I can talk to you until I'm blue in the face and it doesn't do any good.
- If you don't like it, you know where the door is.
- That was stupid.
- What's your problem?
- You think you're always right.
- You don't own me.
- You never help me around the house.
- Who do you think you are?
- You're impossible.
- What do you want now?
- You are such a big baby.
- It's all about you, isn't it?
- How many times do I have to tell you?

Twenty-Five Things Your Husband Longs to Hear

- I've been thinking about you all day.
- What can I do for you today?
- How can I pray for you today?
- The best part of my day is when you come home.
- You are one of God's most precious gifts to me.
- Thank you.
- I'm sorry.
- You are so wonderful.
- You look so handsome today.
- You make my day brighter.
- I don't feel complete without you.
- You are my best friend.
- I love spending time with you.
- Thank you for taking such good care of me.
- You are my knight in shining armor.
- I will always love you.
- I trust your decisions.
- I can always count on you.
- What would you like to do?
- I prize every moment we're together.
- I see God's fingerprints all over you.
- You are such an inspiration to so many people.
- You are such a wonderful father.
- You could give classes on how to be a great husband.
- I believe in you.

*T*HE *P*OWER OF A *W*OMAN'S *W*ORDS TO *H*ER *F*RIENDS

Encouragement is oxygen to the soul.

—GEORGE MATTHEW ADAMS

IT WAS THE WORST phone call of Ann's life.

"Hello."

"Hey, Mom. This is Hugh."

"Hi, son. What are you doing calling me in the middle of the day? Is everything all right?"

"No, it's not. Can you come?"

During the summer after Hugh's freshman year in college, his mom watched helplessly as he sank into a deep depression. A dark cloud engulfed his emotions, and he couldn't see or feel his way out. Ann and her husband took what they felt were positive steps to help, but when they took Hugh back to school the following fall, everything in Ann cried out for her to wrap her arms around her son and keep him under her wing.

Three months later the darkness became so bleak that Hugh knew he was in trouble and checked into a hospital. Trying to be a ray of sunshine to penetrate the darkness, Ann moved into a furnished apartment near his campus and spread her wings as a safe place for him to heal. They finished his semester together.

Why do I tell you this story in a section on friends? Because Ann said she could not have made it through that difficult year without an incredible gift of God...her friend Mary.

"God sent Mary to be His hands and feet, embracing arms, listening ear, and encouraging friend," Ann recalls. "It was Mary who made the hotel reservation for me as we quickly drove to the hospital. It was Mary who cried out to God on our behalf when I was too tired to kneel. It was Mary who reminded me that God was still on His throne and that He was good when I had times of doubt. It was Mary who understood because she had been there herself.

"When I didn't know what was going on in Hugh's mind, Mary could tell me what had transpired in her own," Ann continued. "When Hugh had no hope that life could ever be different than it was at that moment, it was Mary's words, a fellow sojourner and friend, who showed me otherwise. While she encouraged me through e-mails and phone calls, she encouraged Hugh through the words she had penned in her book *Hope in the Midst of Depression*. He might not have believed me, but he believed her because she had traveled through the tunnel and emerged once again into the light. When I felt despair wash over me with its broad brush strokes of gray, Mary assured me that it would lift and the bright colors would eventually return."

Emily Dickinson once said, "Hope is the thing with feathers that perches in the soul—and sings the tune without words—and never stops at all." We can be the voice of hope when a friend forgets the melody of her heart. Mary was that friend for Ann. That is the power of a woman's words to her friends.

Friendship Was God's Idea

We have already seen that God said, "It is not good for the man to be alone" (Genesis 2:18). While He created a woman to be man's completer and companion, He also created women to be in close relationship with other women. We were created in the image of God to be relational beings.

Jesus could very well have come to earth and lived in solitude. And yet He chose to be in relationship with people. He ministered to the masses, but also chose 12 men with whom He nurtured a spiritually intimate relationship. Likewise, I believe that God has designed women to develop godly friendships and encourage each other with our words. We are much like coals or cinders that die out alone, but burst into flame when brought together and stirred.

The prophet Isaiah wrote: "The Sovereign LORD has given me an instructed tongue, to know the word that sustains the weary" (Isaiah 50:4). The words of a woman to her friend can make the difference between victory or defeat.

Throughout Scripture, we see how God placed women together in relationships to encourage one another and provide a place of retreat. Just as God sent Ruth to Naomi and Mary to Elizabeth, He continues to place women together for mutual support, accountability, and friendship. Women are the very heartbeat of the home, community, and church, and many are in desperate need of resuscitation! Let's take a look at a couple of women in the Bible and discover how to use our words to encourage our friends.

Treasured Friends

Naomi was a woman who needed a heaping dose of encouraging words. She was a young girl when she met and married Elimelech. His name meant "God is King," and she knew that he would always serve the living God of Israel. The young couple had two sons, whose names suggested they were somewhat of a disappointment: Mahlon meant "puny or weakling" and Kilion meant "pining."

When the boys were still young lads, a famine struck the area surrounding Bethlehem, and the city whose name meant "House of Bread" had no bread to feed its own. So Elimelech packed up his family of four and headed to Moab in hopes of better days.

We are not sure of the details that followed, but we do know that both boys married Moabite women. Over the next ten years Elimelech, Mahlon, and Kilion died, leaving Naomi alone with her two Moabite daughters-in-law. Downcast, defeated, and discouraged, Naomi decided to return to her homeland and her people. The famine had passed, and even though there was no hope of grandchildren to carry on her family name, or a husband or son to care for her in her twilight years, at least she would be among familiar faces.

> *Learn to greet your friends with a smile. They carry too many frowns in their own hearts to be bothered with yours.*
>
> —MARY ALLETTE AYER

"Girls," Naomi said one day, "I have heard news from my homeland. God has remembered Bethlehem and the famine has passed. There is no reason for me to stay in Moab, and I have decided to return to the land of my people. I want you both to go back to your mother's house and find other nice young men to marry. I pray God will be as kind to you as you have been to me."

Naomi kissed each of the girls as they wept loudly. "We will go back with you to your people," they cried.

"No, my daughters," Naomi said. "Go back home. There's no reason for you to come with me. I know it is the custom for you to marry another son in a family if your husband dies, but I'm not going to have any more sons. Even if I did, I wouldn't want you to wait around until they were old enough to marry. Now, go back to your mother's house. That is the best solution. The Lord's hand has gone out against me. My dreams are buried with Elimelech, Mahlon, and Kilion."

The two women loved their mother-in-law dearly and wept with tears streaming down their cheeks. After what seemed like hours, one of the girls, Orpah, kissed her mother-in-law goodbye and turned to walk away. The other girl, Ruth, clung to Naomi's robe and begged to go with her.

"Don't urge me to leave you or to turn back from you. Where you go I will go, and where you stay I will stay. Your people will be my people and your God my God. Where you die I will die, and there I will be buried. May the LORD deal with me, be it ever so severely, if anything but death separates you and me" (Ruth 1:16-17).

Naomi and Ruth both knew that most Israelites despised Moabites. The Israelites had never forgiven the Moabites for hiring Balaam to place a curse on them after they left Egypt for the Promised Land many years before (Numbers 22:1-6). Yet, regardless of the opposition Ruth knew she would face, she still desired to go and take care of her friend.

So Naomi relented and allowed Ruth to return with her. After the arduous journey, the dusty and exhausted women arrived at their destination. The twosome caused quite a stir, and the townspeople began to whisper among themselves, "Could this be Naomi? It looks like her, and yet it doesn't."

She was so depressed, downcast, and discouraged that her very countenance disguised the woman she had been before. Naomi heard the whispers as she walked by and stopped in her tracks. "Don't call me Naomi [which means pleasant]," she told them. "Call me Mara [which means bitter], because the Almighty has made my life very bitter. I went away full, but the LORD has brought me back empty. Why call me Naomi? The LORD has afflicted me; the Almighty has brought misfortune upon me" (Ruth 1:20-21).

I imagine Ruth felt a pang in her heart at the words "brought me back empty." Part of her must have thought, *What about me?* But the other part knew Naomi was speaking out of her loss and pain. Naomi was blinded by bitterness and didn't recognize hope walking right beside her in the form of a Moabite girl.

All through the book of Ruth we see how God used this daughter-in-law to encourage her forlorn friend. She went out into the field to glean barley to feed her, she lent a listening ear to console her, and she offered words to soothe her. God even used Ruth to jog Naomi's memory and remind her that she was not alone in the world. She had a kinsman-redeemer by the name of Boaz—a distant relative who was more than willing; yes, even eager to care for her. Boaz married the widow Ruth, and together they placed hope in the arms of Naomi...a baby boy by the name of Obed. Maybe you're not familiar with the name Obed, but I bet you've heard of his grandson—the most powerful king in Israel's history, King David.

I suspect that Naomi asked her friends to stop calling her Mara after the marriage of Ruth and the birth of her first grandson. I imagine she reclaimed her title of "pleasant." Her friends proclaimed, "Praise be to the LORD, who this day has not left you without a kinsman-redeemer. May he become famous throughout Israel! He will renew your life and sustain you in your old age. For your daughter-in-law, who loves you and who is better to you than seven sons, has given him birth" (Ruth 4:14-15).

When Naomi returned to town, her old acquaintances were shocked at her downcast appearance. She had gone away married and wealthy, but she returned home widowed and poor. However, we see no signs that they offered to alleviate her pain or minister to her in any way. They wagged their tongues in gossip but did nothing to lighten her load.

On the other hand, Ruth gives us a wonderful example of how to care for a broken-spirited friend. She didn't reprimand Naomi, scold her with words reminding her why she needed to be thankful, or tell her to stop feeling sorry for herself. She didn't berate her with words such as, "You're not the only one suffering around here, you know. I lost my husband too!"

No, Ruth loved Naomi unconditionally, cared for her unceasingly, and supported her unselfishly. Ruth is a wonderful example of Paul's words to the Galatians. "Rejoice with those who rejoice, and weep with those who weep" (Romans 12:15 NASB).

Have you ever noticed that hurting people hurt people? Many times a friend in pain may toss words about like darts, and the whole world becomes the target. A wise woman will extend a hurting friend much grace during such a time, knowing that she is talking through the megaphone of pain. I imagine Ruth endured more than being ignored…perhaps she served as the target for pointed words as well. Yet she was persistent and consistent in her love for Naomi.

Let's look at Galatians 6:2: "Carry each other's burdens." The word "burdens" might more aptly be translated "overburdens."[1] It is more than simply having too many errands to run, a dirty house, or a never-ending pile of laundry. An overburden is when the burdens of life grow too heavy for someone to carry alone, such as the loss of a spouse, the death of a family member, the rebellion of a teen, the termination of a job, or the bad report from a biopsy.

Ruth gives us an example of how to bear someone's burden. She took care of Naomi's emotional needs by simply staying with her, her physical needs by providing food for her, and her spiritual needs by reminding her of the providence of God. It all began with her words—a declaration of determination and love: "Don't urge me to leave you or turn back from you. Where you go I will go, and where you stay

> *A friend is someone who understands your past, believes in your future, and accepts you just the way you are.*
>
> —AUTHOR UNKNOWN

I will stay. Your people will be my people and your God my God. Where you die I will die, and there I will be buried" (Ruth 1:16-17). In other words, "Naomi, I'm not leaving you, so just forget about it. You are my friend, and I'm in this relationship for the long haul. You can't get rid of me by simply moving out of town. I'm coming with you!"

Naomi's circumstances were dire, but any friendship will experience periods when someone hits a dry spell and is not able to give much to the relationship. The test of a true friend is whether or not we can love enough to wait it out. Walter Winchell once said, "A friend is one who walks in when others walk out."

What if a hurting friend shuts you out as Naomi tried to shut her two daughters-in-law out of her life? We can choose, like Orpah, to turn and walk away. Or we can choose, like Ruth, to stick close by.

Ruth was in pain, and yet she was able to focus on her dear friend. She lived up to her name, which means "woman friend." She gives us a vivid example of how to hold an emotional umbrella over a friend through the storms of life.

Tireless Friends

When I was in my teens, I went scuba diving with some friends. I had no training and probably shouldn't have been in deep water, but I was a teenager and threw caution to the wind. The young man who took me below the surface of the deep strapped an oxygen tank on his back, a mask on his face, and flippers on his feet. I only had a mask and flippers.

"Where's my oxygen?" I asked.

"I've got it," he answered as he patted the tank on his back.

So into the ocean we jumped. He put his arm around my waist as though I were a sack of potatoes and down we went. John drew oxygen from the tank and then passed the breathing apparatus to me. We took turns breathing in the oxygen in what he called "buddy breathing." It then occurred to me that I was totally dependent on this young boy to keep me alive!

This was not a very smart idea, but it did leave me with a great life lesson…"Buddy Breathing." Throughout my life, the words of my friends have been like oxygen when I feel as though I'm drowning. Even today, I have a mental scrapbook of the life-giving words passed along to me in the ocean of despair.

In 1974 I traveled to Europe with a group of students to study abroad. My family was falling apart, and yet I felt compelled to leave the safety of my friends to spend 12 weeks with strangers. A big part of me did not want to go. Being a new Christian, I depended on my friends to keep me afloat. However, God was trying to teach me how to swim on my own.

Before I left, my group of Christian girlfriends gave me a gift. They had taken a large medicine bottle and filled it with a homemade remedy. A handwritten label was taped to the outside with the following instructions:

For: Miss Sharon Edwards PBP 71240
Take as needed for uplifting of the spirit.
May be followed by faith and prayer for faster relief.
Vitamin PTLa
Filled by SIC

Inside the medicine bottle were 100 Bible verses written on small strips of paper and rolled up like tiny scrolls. These verses were my medicine. The "pharmacists" were my Sisters in Christ, and the Vitamins were Praise the Lord anyway brand. That gift of the heart was given to me more than 30 years ago, and yet I've carried them with me through high school, college, marriage, and many, many moves. I have kept that bottle of love with me at each crossroad and bend in the road. That's the power of a woman's words to her friends. We never know how a small act of kindness will touch someone's heart for many years to come.

Kim discovered this simple fact when she was sinking to the bottom of her emotional sea. "I was probably at the lowest place emotionally and spiritually I had been since asking Jesus into my heart," Kim explained. "I call it my 'tomb time,' a time of loneliness, darkness, and death."

God seemed distant and aloof to Kim, and life was just not turning out like she had hoped. She doubted her abilities, her faith, and her interpersonal relationships.

"During this period, I ran into an old friend I hadn't seen for a while," Kim continued. "I admired her so much. Sue was a few years older than me, and just the kind of woman I always wanted to be. She noticed my sad countenance and asked what was going on in my life. I shared the details of my pain, and she wrapped me in her arms and in prayer."

A few days later Kim received a letter from Sue. She quoted Isaiah 42:3: "A bruised reed He will not break and a dimly burning wick He will not extinguish" (NASB). At the bottom of the letter Sue wrote four simple, powerful words: "I believe in you."

"I wept when I read those words," Kim remembered. "Amazingly, tears still swell when I think of her words today. I couldn't believe in myself, but this woman, whom I loved and admired, believed in me. Those words set me on a course of hope that somehow life would get better...and it did. God is faithful and I am so grateful He sent Sue to give me hope. Even today, when I feel bruised or that my light is a bit dim, I sense God's hands surrounding me to keep me from breaking or my little light from blowing out, and I remember that my dear friend believes in me. God's hands and Sue's heart—that's all I need to press on until the sun shines again. I remember the power of those words, and I have spoken and written them to others, hoping they too will be encouraged to press on."

As Kim told me her story, tears brimmed in her eyes. The incident occurred 17 years ago. Words have lasting impact, my friend. Lasting impact.

True Friends

We have looked at various aspects of the words of a woman to her friends. What I've noticed through the years is that a true friend is one who knows what I need without me even asking. She is someone who will offer to pitch in and help when she sees me growing weary. A true friend never sees the mess in my house, but the love in my eyes. She listens without judging, but sets me straight when she sees me straying off course. She never ridicules my children or my husband, and encourages me to love them better. She doesn't simply say, "I'll pray for you," but rather, "Let's stop and pray right now."

A true friend says, "I believe in you, and I'll be the first to blow the horn at your celebration party!"

King Solomon painted a beautiful portrait of the power of a woman's words to her friends in Ecclesiastes 4:9-10,12:

> Two are better than one, because they have a good return for
> their labor: If they fall down, they can help each other up.
> But pity those who fall and have no one to help them up!...
> A cord of three strands is not quickly broken (TNIV).

We can embrace a friend with words that warm a chilled soul, words that fill an empty heart, and words that lift her up when she is lying face down in defeat.

Toppled Friends

It was just a bit of burlap peeking out from underneath the soil, but to our golden retriever, Ginger, it was a challenge that needed to be pursued.

Shortly after we had planted a maple tree in our backyard, we went on vacation. It was the first time we had left Ginger home alone, and a neighbor fed and watched out for her while we were away. On the second day of our trip, I called Cathy to see how our pet was faring.

"Well, Ginger's fine," Cathy reported. "But you know that tree you planted last week? She dug it up!"

"She did what!" I exclaimed.

"She dug it up. The tree is lying in the yard on its side."

When we got home, we assessed the situation. It seemed that when we planted the tree, we left a small piece of the burlap around the root ball exposed. Ginger spied that remnant peeking out of the ground and wanted it...bad. A few times we had caught her pawing at the burlap, reprimanded her with a stern no, and she had walked away. I imagine that the moment she saw us pull out of the driveway with a packed car she crept over to the forbidden tree and began to dig. She must have dug and dug for hours with all her puppy might—flinging dirt in every direction. *I've got to get to the bottom of this,* she might have thought. *This must be exposed!*

Finally, she accomplished her mission and the burlap was totally uncovered! Exposed! Of course, she gave no thought to the tree she toppled in the meantime. It was never about the tree.

> A man (woman) never discloses his (her) own character so clearly as when he (she) describes another's.
>
> —JEAN PAUL RICHTER

As I stared at the poor little maple lying helplessly in the yard in the hot drying sun, I thought about how many friends I've observed in the same state. I thought about friends I have known, and myself, for that matter, who have been toppled for much the same reason. Perhaps someone has a little flaw that comes to the surface in plain view. Then someone else comes along and decides that the flaw is a nuisance and must be exposed at all cost. Someone starts digging and digging—flinging dirt in every direction with no thought to what all the digging is doing to the friend. The rough burlap may be unearthed, but unfortunately the friend lies toppled in the process.

Lifeless, wounded, exposed—and for what purpose? To satisfy someone's dogged determination to uncover a rough edge?

There are times in any friendship when confrontation is necessary, but we must always make sure that the confrontation is wrapped in prayer and tied with the lovely bow of love. If we take any joy whatsoever in the process, then we must stop and check our motives and attitude.

Ann Hibbard, in her book *Treasured Friends,* describes the difference between a friend who tends to dig us up and one who longs to hold us up:

A true friend is someone we look to for support. She is always on our team, cheering us on to victory. When we have a problem, she does not try to solve it for us. Instead, she listens and expresses her solidarity. When our perspective has become distorted by self-pity, she encourages us, not with pat answers but by gently pointing us toward the truth.

There is never a hint of criticism from a true friend. That doesn't mean she doesn't sometimes say hard things. She is the one who asks the tough questions. But we know that her intentions for us are only good. Anyone can say what we want to hear. A true friend tells us what we need to hear. Yet, every word is prompted by love.[2]

Steve and I gently removed what was left of the burlap sack around the root system, carefully sat the maple back up into her prepared soil, and lovingly patted the dirt back around her parched roots. Then, because of her weakened state, we braced her up with ropes tied to three stakes in the ground. I watered the weary maple daily, not knowing if she would recover from the trauma. In the end, the tree not only survived, she thrived.

Oh, that we would do the same for our toppled friends. When we see a friend who has been wounded by words, we can slowly stand her back up, lovingly reestablished her roots in the good soil of God's Word, gently brace her up with kindness, and water her daily with prayer. Who knows? You may even help her not only survive, but thrive.

Thankfully, Ginger left the tree alone after that episode. After all—she never cared about the tree in the first place.

Tenderly Tenacious Friends

Dale Carnegie, author of *How to Win Friends and Influence People*, said, "You can make more friends in two months by becoming interested in other people than you can in two years by trying to get people interested in you." Everyone has an inborn need to feel significant. When we listen to a friend and engage in conversation with questions that show we're interested in their lives, then that person feels esteemed and that they matter in this world. The Bible teaches, "Let us consider how we may spur one another on toward love and good deeds" (Hebrews 10:24).

In my silverware drawer at home, I have about 15 knives of various shapes and sizes. However, I only use about four of them, and the others simply are taking up space. The problem is, the other knives are dull and I've never taken the time to sharpen them. I could just toss them in the trash, but that seems like such a waste.

The same can be true in our own lives. The Bible says, "As iron sharpens iron, so one person sharpens another" (Proverbs 27:17 TNIV). When we don't have friends that challenge us and encourage us to grow, we become dull. Ultimately, we become "not the sharpest knife in the drawer," and others are chosen for tasks that we would love to do. Is there someone God is calling you to sharpen? Is there someone whom God is nudging you to invite to be a sharpening agent?

Jesus gave us a word of caution when it comes to "sharpening" our friends. Do it in love. Alice Miller has a good rule of thumb for correction: "If it is very painful for you to criticize your friends, you are safe in doing it. But if you take the slightest pleasure in it, that is the time to hold your tongue."

Bonnie is one of my friends who keeps me sharp. Her some-times brutal honesty is couched in such love for me that I can take the sharpening stone even if it hurts. It is a tough love that I have grown to appreciate and admire. Sometimes her honesty makes me burst out laughing.

Bonnie lives in Michigan and I live in North Carolina. Because I am a writer and she works for a publishing house, we frequently attend the same conventions. Bonnie and I take every opportunity to visit, and we room together at many of these meetings. One night, after an exhausting day of meetings, Bonnie and I were snuggled in our adjacent beds chatting. I confided in her about an internal struggle I was having with a particular person.

"That's just plain old sin," Bonnie said.

"What?" I asked

"Sharon, that's sin. You need to pray about that," she flatly replied.

I have to tell you, I laughed till I cried. Who else but Bonnie would call a spade and spade and label my whining for exactly what it was? I love her to pieces. She's not afraid to pull out the sharpening stone when she notices I'm getting a bit dull.

But everyone can't be a Bonnie in our lives. She has earned the right to sharpen me because she loves me well. Likewise, we can't go around expecting to use our words to sharpen others around us without loving them first. Otherwise, the words will have destructive power and will not be received at all.

As women, we love to soak in warm bubble baths, lather in fragrant soaps, and soften with aromatic oils. But all too often, when it comes to removing dirt from a friend, we pull out the hard-bristled scrub brush of harsh words and scrub, scrub, scrub. The end result is often not the removal of dirt, but a wounded, scraped, and bruised soul. Powerful words are not caustic words. They are gentle, tender words wrapped in an attitude of love. Paul wrote to the Colossians, "As God's chosen people, holy and dearly loved, clothe yourselves with compassion, kindness, humility, gentleness and patience" (Colossians 3:12).

We all make mistakes. The prophet Isaiah wrote, "We all, like sheep, have gone astray" (Isaiah 53:6). The composer Beethoven said it this way: "We all make mistakes, but everyone makes different mistakes." The philosopher Goethe remarked, "One has only to grow older to become more tolerant. I see no fault that I might not have committed myself."

If we feel that we must use our words to exhort or correct a friend, we should be keenly aware that there are most likely areas in our own lives that need correcting as well. Jesus said, "Why do you look at the speck of sawdust in your brother's eye and pay no attention to the plank in your own eye? How can you say to your brother, 'Let me take the speck out of your eye,' when all the time there is a plank in your own eye? You hypocrite, first take the plank out of your own eye, and then you will see clearly to remove the speck from your brother's eye" (Matthew 7:3-5).

I am not suggesting that we withhold the sharpening tool when it is needed, but just make sure it is well oiled with love and a gentle spirit before the rub begins.

Timely Friends

My son was fast, and he ran with a fast crowd. As a matter of fact, his entire track team was pretty fast! In the ninth grade, Steven participated in the conference track meet, running the 1600 meters. (That's four times around the big circle.) I was so proud of him as he ran like a gazelle around the first lap, about six feet behind the first-place participant. But, at some point during the beginning of the second lap we saw an unidentified flying object soar over Steven's head.

"What was that?" my husband asked. "It's a bird. It's a plane. No, it's Steven's shoe!"

All the fans were laughing and pointing as they noticed Steven's left running shoe fly heavenward and land on the grassy field. But amazingly, Steven kept running and never missed a beat. With one shoe off and one shoe on, he continued running. The atmosphere of the race sparked with excitement and the focus seemed to change. It became less about who would win and more about if Steven would make it to the finish line. All curious eyes were now on one lean runner. Would he stop? Would he slow down? Would his sock stay on?

His teammates began to run around the track, cheering him on. "Come on, Steven! Don't give up! Don't slow down! Keep going!"

Surprisingly, at the urging of his teammates, Steven sped up. By the third lap, he had passed the first-place runner by several paces. But then, predictably, his sock started to work its way down the ankle and the toe was flopping like a loose sole of a worn old shoe. Undaunted, Steven ran on, sock flopping behind.

When Steven crossed the finish line in first place, the crowd erupted in applause and laughter. He had broken his personal best running time!

"Son, maybe you should have kicked off both shoes. No tellin' what you could have done," my husband cheered. "You made your best time ever. What made the difference?"

"I knew everybody was looking at me," Steven answered. "It wasn't just a race anymore; they were watching to see what I'd do. It made me go faster. It made me want to do better."

All through our lives, we will notice "fellow runners" who have lost more than a shoe—they have lost their hopes, their dreams, and their will to finish the race. What will we do? What can we do? We can cheer them on by offering a timely word of encouragement and running alongside them shouting, "Come on, friend! Don't give up! Don't slow down! Keep going!"

Who knows, that friend may do more than simply finish the race. She may even take first place!

Types of Friends

One day I conducted an experiment. Actually, it was not intentional, but I learned a valuable lesson. I send out online devotions to people who sign up to receive them on my website. I write them and my husband proofs them before they go out. However, on this particular day, I was in a hurry and sent it to my webmaster before even reading through the words a second time or giving it to Steve to proof. I was horrified when I later read the posted devotion smattered with typos. *Oh, well,* I thought as I humbly clicked the devotion off. "Grace, grace, grace," as my friend Mary Southerland always says.

But the interesting part was the responses I got from the devotion. One woman wrote back, "Check your spelling! Run a grammar check!" Another woman wrote back, "Today's devotion meant so much to me. Thank you for ministering to me through your words."

Then another wrote, "Sharon, I just hate to see typos in your wonderful devotions. I know you are busy. Here's an idea. Why don't you send your devotions to me and I will proof them for you?"

As I looked at those e-mails, I saw the power of a woman's words to our friends encapsulated in those three responses.

- One woman simply pointed out my faults.

- One woman overlooked my faults and encouraged me in the ways I had been a blessing to her.

- One woman encouraged me, acknowledged my errors, and then went one step further. She offered to help.

What a great accidental experiment! We can be one of those three types of friends. We can be the type who simply points out faults, the type who overlooks the faults and focuses on the positives, or the type who praises someone's strengths and offers to help when there is a weakness.

A Walk Down Friendship Lane

Even when I'm tucked away on my patio behind my house, I can tell when a neighbor is going for a walk or a jogger is running down the street. It starts with Mitzi, the white cockapoo one block away. Yip. Yip. Yip. Then it moves two houses down with Duchess, the black Labrador. Bow. Wow. Wow. The wave continues to move closer with Pal, the standard poodle. Arf. Arf. Arf. And onto Sprout, the collie. Woof. Woof. Woof.

Finally, the pedestrian turns off Stratfordshire Drive onto my side street, Trafalgar. All of a sudden, the doggie hallelujah chorus breaks out with Alice, the white Lab, and Maple, the Heinz 57 across the street, and Duchess, the German shepherd next door. I usually don't see the passerby, but I can surely hear the snarles and insults from the dogs as he or she strolls along.

When I take my routine three-mile walk through the neighborhood I am also greeted by the wave of barking dogs indignant that I should dare pass by their turf. I try not to let it hurt my feelings. However, the chain reaction of barking, jeering, growling, and gnashing of teeth never ceases to unnerve me.

The truth is, I wish the pups would wag their tails as I walk by as if to say, "Oh, there's that sweet Mrs. Jaynes. My, how I like her. I wish she were my master and we could take walks together. Mrs. Jaynes! Mrs. Jaynes! Won't you please come over and pat my head?" I wish they would run up to the fence, jump up sweetly, and rest their paws, beckoning me to stop for a visit. But for the 20 years I walked the same route, this has never happened. It's always growl, ruff, and bark. You'd think I'd get used to the barking, but I never do.

The reason a dog has so many friends is because he wags his tail instead of his tongue.

—Author Unknown

I hate to admit it, but it's been the same way in life from time to time. As I've walked down the path of years, especially down that road less traveled, I have heard some unfriendly barking, some disapproving jeering, and a few disdainful growls. Sometimes it's a complaint because I'm not living up to someone's expectations. Sometimes it's because I'm not following someone else's plan for my life. And sometimes it's because I'm coloring outside people-imposed lines.

But let's just stop and call it what it is. Barking. Yapping. Howling.

Thankfully, among the barking from the dogs during my neighborhood stroll are friendly salutations from neighbors and passersby. "Good morning, Sharon" a friend calls out from watering her garden. "Have a good day," a neighbor calls as she passes by on her way to work. "Hi, Mrs. Jaynes," a boy shouts as he speeds by on his bike. These are the words I treasure along the way.

As friends, we have the opportunity to cheer someone on during their busy day or simply bark, yap, and howl. A good friend will not tear someone down with her tongue but build her up with positive words as they walk along life's journey together.

I have often heard that there are two types of people: those that brighten a room when they enter and those that brighten a room when they leave. The barking, whiny ones take the dark cloud with them when they leave. The positive, cheery ones reflect God's light when they arrive. Which one are you? Simply take a look at the faces of the people around you when you walk into a room. If you're not getting the response you hoped for, reevaluate your words and attitude. God is all about change!

POWER-PACKED WORDS

Words a Friend Would Love to Hear

Jesus taught, "Treat others as you want them to treat you" (Luke 6:31 TLB). Make a list of words that *you* would like to hear and then use those same words to bless others. If there are words you would like to hear, chances are there are others out there who would like to hear them too.

Below are some of my favorites:

- You bring out the best in me.
- You are an inspiration to me.
- I love to hear how God is working in your life.
- How can I pray for you today?
- I can help you with that.
- I'd like your opinion.
- What do you think?
- You teach me so much about friendship.
- You inspire me to be a better person.

- You are a great wife, mother, friend, etc.
- Can I bring dinner to you tonight?
- I believe in you.
- You can accomplish anything God has called you to do.
- I am so glad we are friends.
- Yep, you made a mistake. Now, let's put it behind us and move on.
- You won't see me throwing the first stone.
- We all make mistakes.
- Thank you for...
- I am hurting with you.
- I don't understand either.
- Will you help me _____? You are so good at it.
- What can I do to help you reach your goal?
- You are such a great friend.
- I have learned so much from you.
- I want to be like you when I grow up.

*T*HE *P*OWER OF A *W*OMAN'S *W*ORDS TO *F*ELLOW *B*ELIEVERS

The world at its worst needs the church at its best.

—AUTHOR UNKNOWN

A WOMAN CALLED Butterball Turkey's consumer hotline and asked about the advisability of cooking a turkey that had been in her freezer for 23 years. The customer service representative told her that it might be okay to eat it if the freezer had maintained a below-zero temperature the entire time, but even so the flavor would have deteriorated so much that it wouldn't be very tasty. Then the caller said, "Oh, that's what we thought. We'll just donate it to the church."

Many times we tend to give "leftovers" to the church or fellow brothers and sisters in Christ, but when it comes to encouraging words, Paul tells us believers need them most of all. "As occasion and opportunity open to us, let us do good [morally] to all people [not only being useful or profitable to them, but also doing what is for their spiritual good and advantage]. Be mindful to be a blessing, *especially to those of the household of faith* [those who belong to God's family with you, the believers]" (Galatians 6:10 AMP). In his letters to the churches of the New Testament, Paul reminded Christians to use their words to build up the body of Christ because he knew how easily we tend to tear it down.

Paul's Pep Talks

When I think of Paul, I tend to think of a stoic stern rock of a man who is neither swayed nor deterred from the course at hand. I see him needing no one other than Christ Himself. But that was not true! Paul needed the encouragement of other believers. He longed for the words of fellow Christians to cheer him on while spreading the gospel.

Ponder these words he penned to the Corinthian church:

> When we came into Macedonia, this body of ours had no rest, but we were harassed at every turn—*conflicts on the outside, fears within.* But God, who comforts the downcast, comforted us by the coming of Titus, and not only by his coming but also by the comfort you had given him. He told us about your longing for me, your deep sorrow, your ardent concern for me, so that my joy was greater than ever (2 Corinthians 7:5-7).

What was Paul feeling at this time? Conflicts on the outside and fears on the inside. Yes, that mighty man of God who said, "I can do everything through him who gives me strength" (Philippians 4:13) also struggled with fear, discouragement, and inner turmoil.

Paul was a spiritually confident man. He wrote: "We are hard pressed on every side, but not crushed; perplexed, but not in despair; persecuted, but not abandoned; struck down, but not destroyed" (2 Corinthians 4:8). "Who shall separate us from the love of Christ? Shall trouble or hardship or persecution or famine or nakedness or danger or sword?…No, in all these things we are more than conquerors through him who loved us" (Romans 8:35-37). Paul believed these words with all of his heart, and yet he still needed the words of fellow believers to encourage him to press on.

Even as I write these words, I am struck with just how much fellow Christians need encouraging words to continue in the faith. It is easy to say, "Well, God should be enough. People should find their strength in Christ." Yes, Christ is enough for salvation. However, God has placed us in a body. He called us the body of Christ because we are dependent on each other to function well, to love well, to struggle well.

"I had worked all year long on the women's retreat," Ann explained. "I didn't get a paycheck, but that wasn't what I was doing it for in the first place. I was planning the retreat to honor Jesus. I'll admit, though, that I longed for someone to tell me 'I appreciate all your hard work,' or 'You really ministered to me,' or 'Thank you for all you do to encourage women.' I didn't do all that work for a pat on the back, but a pat on the back would have meant so much." Then she concluded, "I'm not sure I have it in me to do it again."

I wonder if a few positive words of thanks would have given Ann the fuel she needed to tackle the women's retreat for another year. While the women who attended were filled, Ann left drained and discouraged.

Take a look at how Paul used his words to encourage the various churches in the New Testament:

> I thank my God every time I remember you. In all my prayers for all of you, I always pray with joy because of your partnership in the gospel from the first day until now, being confident of this, that he who began a good work in you will carry it on to completion until the day of Christ Jesus. It is right for me to feel this way about all of you, since I have you in my heart; for whether I am in chains or defending and confirming the gospel, all of you share in God's grace with me. God can testify how I long for all of you with the affection of Christ Jesus. And this is my prayer: that your love may abound more and more in knowledge and depth of insight, so that you may be able to discern

what is best and may be pure and blameless until the day of Christ, filled with the fruit of righteousness that comes through Jesus Christ—to the glory and praise of God (Philippians 1:3-11).

We always thank God, the Father of our Lord Jesus Christ, when we pray for you, because we have heard of your faith in Christ Jesus and of the love you have for all the saints—the faith and love that spring from the hope that is stored up for you in heaven and that you have already heard about in the word of truth, the gospel that has come to you. All over the world this gospel is bearing fruit and growing, just as it has been doing among you since the day you heard it and understood God's grace in all its truth. You learned it from Epaphras, our dear fellow servant, who is a faithful minister of Christ on our behalf, and who also told us of your love in the Spirit (Colossians 1:3-8).

Now look at Paul's words of encouragement to one particular fellow believer, Timothy:

I thank God, whom I serve, as my forefathers did, with a clear conscience, as night and day I constantly remember you in my prayers. Recalling your tears, I long to see you, so that I may be filled with joy (2 Timothy 1:3-4).

Simple words, but powerful words. I imagine Timothy, as well as the churches in Philippi and Colossae, read those words time and time again. Not only did Paul show us how to use our words to spur on fellow believers, he reminded others how to use their words as well. He wrote to Timothy, "Set an example for the believers in *speech,* in life, in love, in faith and in purity" (1 Timothy 4:12).

The Unsuspecting Bride

I ran into Shelly at the grocery store. She had just returned from a visit with her prospective daughter-in-law. Her son was getting married in a few months, and the weekend was intended to help the two families become better acquainted.

"I will tell you one thing," Shelly began. "She might be a Christian, but there is one chapter in the Bible that girl has not read...Proverbs 31. She doesn't know the first thing about how to be a wife. And I know where she got it from. Her mother. Her mother drove us around town and made the men sit in the back. She made all the decisions. It was her show. All weekend it was evident that the women in this family were in charge." Shelly continued pointing out the shortcomings of the bride as I grew more uncomfortable by the minute. My heart went out to her...the bride. This young gal had no idea that her mother-in-law had already decided that she was subpar for her son.

Then Jesus reminded me how hurt He feels when people talk poorly about His bride—the church. And most of the time, the ill-spoken words are within the family itself.

Jesus knew the propensity of His followers to speak unkindly among and about each other. He also knew the destructive potential of our words to turn others away from the faith. Jesus said, "A new command I give you: Love one another. As I have loved you, so you must love one another. *By this all men will know that you are my disciples,* if you love one another" (John 13:34-35). In Jesus' final words before His arrest, He prayed that we would have unity. "My prayer is not for them alone. I pray also for those who will believe in me through their message, that all of them may be one, Father, just as you are in me and I am in you. May they also be in us so that the world may believe that you have sent me" (John 17:20-21).

Others in the Bible instructed us not to speak ill of the bride, but to speak words of love. At least 55 times the words "one another" appear in the Bible. Here are just a few:

- Be devoted to one another in brotherly love. Honor one another above yourselves (Romans 12:10).

- Live in harmony with one another (Romans 12:16).

- Accept one another, then, just as Christ accepted you, in order to bring praise to God (Romans 15:7).

- Encourage one another daily, as long as it is called Today, so that none of you may be hardened by sin's deceitfulness (Hebrews 3:13).

- Be completely humble and gentle; be patient, bearing with one another in love (Ephesians 4:2).

- Be kind and compassionate to one another, forgiving each other, just as in Christ God forgave you (Ephesians 4:32).

- Bear with each other and forgive whatever grievances you may have against one another. Forgive as the Lord forgave you (Colossians 3:13).

- Encourage one another and build each other up, just as in fact you are doing (1 Thessalonians 5:11).

Did you notice how many of these "one anothers" involved words? God has called us to live in community and to use our words to build up each other rather than tear each other down.

Deborah Leads the Way

Women leaders in the Bible are few and far between. However, Deborah's story in the fourth chapter of the book of Judges is enough to make any woman proud.

Deborah was a prophetess who led Israel during a time when her people were being oppressed by the pagan king of Canaan. Her name meant "bee," and she was a busy bee indeed. She served as counselor, judge, and warrior. Deborah held court under a palm tree which became known as the palm of Deborah. The *NIV Study Bible* says this about Deborah and her tree: "The Hebrew word for 'honey' refers to both bees' honey and the sweet syrupy juice of dates. Deborah, the Bee, dispensed the sweetness of justice as she held court, not in a city gate where male judges sat, but under the shade of a 'honey' tree."[1]

I just love that! Many times when I am flitting around like a busy bee, my words are not exactly categorized as honey. As a matter of fact, the busier I get, the more tense and terse my words tend to turn. But not Deborah. Her words were pleasant as a honeycomb and sweet to the soul (Proverbs 16:24).

One day Deborah called for Barak, one of the leaders of the Israeli army. God had given her instructions for this mighty warrior, whose name meant "thunderbolt." As he approached the tree, she passed along his marching orders directly from his Commanding Officer...God.

> The LORD, the God of Israel, commands you: "Go, take with you ten thousand men of Naphtali and Zebulun and lead the way to Mount Tabor. I will lure Sisera, the commander of Jabin's army, with his chariots and his troops to the Kishon River and give him into your hands" (Judges 4:6-7).

Barak cowered at God's command, and like a little boy he said, "If you go with me, I will go; but if you don't go with me, I won't go" (Judges 4:8).

"Very well," Deborah said, "I will go with you. But because of the way you are going about this, the honor will not be yours, for the LORD will hand Sisera over to a woman" (Judges 7:9). (Deborah was not talking about herself, but another woman who would play a major role in the enemies' ultimate defeat. See Judges 4:17-24.) Apparently Barak did not trust in the power of God and insisted that this woman of faith accompany him onto the battlefield.

Deborah reprimanded Barak for his lack of faith, but she did not shame him or step in and do his job for him. She acknowledged that he was the warrior who was to lead the men into battle, and she was the prophetess who was to encourage and inspire. Deborah didn't take the lead, but rather worked with Barak to accomplish God's goals. She accompanied him to the battlefield, and when it came time for the attack, she spurred him on with encouraging words.

"Go! This is the day the LORD has given Sisera into your hands. Has not the LORD gone ahead of you?" (Judges 4:14).

In those days, a king led the way onto battle and the army followed closely behind. Deborah assured Barak that the King of the universe was leading the way and he had only to follow the Lord into victory.

Barak was inspired by this amazing woman. She pumped courage into his failing heart, and he did indeed follow God into battle. She taught him not to focus on the nine hundred iron chariots of the opponent, but on the mighty arm of God. That day, the Lord confused Sisera, and Israel easily routed their enemy. Afterward, Deborah and Barak sang a duet celebrating the nation's victory.

What can we learn from the power of Deborah's words? Her encouragement spurred Barak to become all God had called him to be. She not only gave him the gift of encouraging words, but she walked with him to the battlefield as well. Her words not only bolstered Barak's courage, but also stoked the smoldering embers of the entire army. She stayed true to her calling as an encourager and helped Barak stay true to his as a warrior. She didn't try to be a one-woman show but worked with others to fulfill God's purposes. Going back to chapter 5, Deborah was a true *ezer* who used her words well. Oh, that our words and actions among warriors in the church would be the same!

Miriam Stops the Progress

Now that we have looked at a woman who used her words wisely among God's people, let's flip the coin and look at one who did not...Miriam.

Miriam was the brave little girl who hid among the reeds to watch her baby brother floating in the Nile among the crocodiles and would-be assassins of the Hebrew babies. Because the Hebrews were growing too numerous for Pharaoh's comfort, he issued an edict that all Hebrew male babies must be killed as soon as they were born. But Moses' mother had a dream that her son would live. After she could no longer hide the growing babe in the quiet of her cottage, she wove him his own little ark of reeds, covered it with pitch, and set him afloat in the river.

Miriam watched as Pharaoh's daughter spied the basket and her attendant drew the beautiful boy from the water's edge. "This must be one of the Hebrew babies," she said.

Then Miriam emerged from her hiding place and bravely inquired, "Shall I go and fetch one of the Hebrew women to nurse the baby for you?"

Not only did Moses' mother get to nurse her son and watch him say his first words and toddle his first steps, she was paid handsomely to do so.

Eighty years later, we meet Miriam again. Only this time she is not hiding among the reeds of the Nile, but leading the fleeing Israelites in praise and worship after their escape from Egyptian bondage. Miriam, like Deborah, is also called a prophetess (Exodus 15:20). She used her words to encourage God's people and her musical talents to lead them in song.

But something happened to Miriam along her journey to the Promised Land. She became disgruntled with Moses' leadership and began to use her words to attack her brother rather than attend to God's people. Let's join Miriam as her words became her undoing.

> Miriam and Aaron began to talk against Moses because of his Cushite wife, for he had married a Cushite. "Has the LORD spoken only through Moses?" they asked. "Hasn't he also spoken through us?" And the LORD heard this. (Now Moses was a very humble man, more humble than anyone else on the face of the earth.) At once the LORD

said to Moses, Aaron and Miriam, "Come out to the Tent of Meeting, all three of you." So the three of them came out. Then the LORD came down in a pillar of cloud; he stood at the entrance to the Tent and summoned Aaron and Miriam. When both of them stepped forward, he said, "Listen to my words:

When a prophet of the LORD is among you, I reveal myself to him in visions, I speak to him in dreams. But this is not true of my servant Moses; he is faithful in all my house. With him I speak face to face, clearly and not in riddles; he sees the form of the LORD. Why then were you not afraid to speak against my servant Moses?" (Numbers 12:1-8).

Those are words that should strike fear into any of us who dare to speak against God's children. We should be *afraid* to speak against God's elect. As Paul wrote, "Who are you to judge someone else's servant? To his own master he stands or falls. And he will stand, for the Lord is able to make him stand" (Romans 14:4).

When the cloud from which God spoke to Miriam and Aaron lifted, Miriam was covered in leprosy and her skin appeared like snow. Moses, even though he was the one questioned and ridiculed, prayed for God to heal his sister. Yes, God did heal her leprous skin and her diseased words, but not before she spent seven days in isolation outside the camp. Ultimately, more than a million people's journey came to a halt for a week because of one woman's sin. Her grumbling, gossiping words impeded the entire group from heading to where God had intended them to go.

Have you experienced a similar situation? A situation in which one person's words or a group of people's words brought God's work to a sudden stop?

All too often the church becomes a breeding ground for grumbling and gossiping. Church members have very specific ideas about how a church should be run: contemporary music vs. traditional music, choir robes vs. street clothes, seeker-sensitive vs. discipleship of believers. Before you know it, the journey to the Promised Land comes to a halt.

Miriam was not the only one who grumbled among those headed toward the Promised Land. God cared for the Israelites by His own hand—providing water from a rock, manna from heaven, quail from the sky, clothes that never wore out, a fire by night, and a cloud by day. And yet they grumbled. Do you think they all started grumbling at once? I don't. I think it started with a few murmurs and grew like an approaching train.

Back in the late '50s, there was a movie called *The Blob*. The blob looked like a massive pile of silly putty that rolled along swallowing up everything and everyone in its path. That's what grumbling and gossiping can do among believers. It also rolls along, swallowing up unsuspecting victims along the way.

God didn't take too kindly to Miriam's grumbling. While she started out whispering about Moses' choice of a wife, that was not really the issue at all. It was jealousy, pure and simple. Actually, there was nothing "pure" about it.

"Has the LORD spoken only through Moses? Hasn't he also spoken through us?" Her words and attitude of jealousy were just as destructive to the cause of God as the infectious leprosy that ate away at her fingers and toes. Why was only Miriam punished and not Aaron? I imagine that she was the principle instigator of the ill-spoken words and Aaron happened to be in the blob's path.

Let's back up to Numbers 12:3: "Now Moses was a very humble man, more humble than anyone else on the face of the earth." Some theologians suggest that the word "miserable" is a better translation of the Hebrew word than "humble." "Ever since Numbers 11:1, one thing after another had brought pressure on Moses so that in 11:14 he whimpers to God that he is not able to bear the load any longer. He even asks that he might die to be relieved of the pressures. Now with this assault of his sister and brother, it was simply too much. He was now the most 'miserable' man on the earth. He had found his lot so difficult, his task so unmanageable, his pressure so intense that he called out to God saying, 'It is too much!' (11:4) 'Now the man Moses was exceedingly miserable, more than any man on the face of the earth!'"[2]

When someone is bending under the pressure of trying to please God and the grumblers he or she is trying to serve, what is needed is not more booing and hissing from the crowd, but cheers and holy pep talks from the team. "Do all things without grumbling," Paul encourages the church at Philippi (Philippians 2:14 NASB). Encourage one another...

We have a choice. We can be a Deborah, who dispenses encouragement from the honey tree and walks side by side with Christian soldiers into battle. Or we can be a Miriam, who stirs up strife and causes the march to the Promised Land (or wherever God is leading) to come to a complete stop.

A Modern-Day Miriam

It was not a speaking engagement I was looking forward to. A few weeks prior to the event, a woman in the church stirred up a heap of trouble. She had read one of my books and taken great issue with the principle of a wife submitting to her husband. She didn't believe in submission and was so offended that I would suggest the idea that she went to the pastor and complained about their choice of a speaker.

"I can't believe you would invite this woman to speak at this church. I don't agree with her principles. Have you read her books?" the woman asked.

"No, I haven't," the pastor answered. "They are for women, and I, being a man, haven't read them."

The woman continued to speak caustic words that were filtered through past hurts in her own life. The pastor trusted the women's ministry leadership team, but the woman's words planted seeds of doubt in his mind.

The leadership team never intended for me to discover the little storm brewing around my arrival, but nevertheless the whirlwind reached my ears. My prayer team blasted the gates of heaven with prayers to abate the spiritual warfare that was following me to the doors of this church.

It was a sellout event and had to be moved to a different building because of the overflow. Sixteen women came to Christ that night. God won the battle, but there were bleeding souls left in the aftermath of this modern-day Miriam.

The women's ministry director resigned, feelings were hurt, and the women's ministry team's decisions were questioned. The entire women's ministry department fell apart, and no one wanted to step in and face the possibility of that type of ridicule and dissension. The church's journey to their Promised Land was halted for a time.

All from the words of one woman. Oh, dear ones, there is so much power in our words! May we use them to encourage one another in what God has called us to do rather than throw up roadblocks to halt the spiritual progress of our brothers and sisters in Christ.

Refreshment for the Refreshers

A few years ago Mary Johnson, a friend of mine, had a significant, time-consuming role in making stage props and decorations for the church Christmas program. She worked for months on white flowing robes, sparkling sheer backdrops, and frosted glittery stage props. The church was transformed into a picturesque heavenly wonderland that took our imaginations to a different world. Well over 2000 people viewed the Christmas program and marveled at Mary's handiwork. And what did Mary receive for all her effort? One note of thanks.

"Of course, I didn't do the work to get accolades or pats on the back," Mary told me later. "But I read that one note over and over again."

I deeply regret that I did not write that note.

Many times a word of thanks or appreciation is the only reward a fellow believer in Christ receives this side of heaven. The writer of Proverbs wrote, "He who refreshes others will himself be refreshed"

God's Garden

In growing a healthy, fruit-bearing church, try this plan:

Plant three rows of squash:

- Squash gossip.
- Squash criticism.
- Squash indifference.

Plant seven rows of peas:

- Prayer
- Promptness
- Perseverance
- Politeness
- Preparedness
- Purity
- Patience

Plant seven heads of lettuce:

- Let us be unselfish and loyal.
- Let us be faithful to duty.
- Let us search the Scriptures.
- Let us not be weary in well-doing.
- Let us be truthful.
- Let us love one another.[3]

(Proverbs 11:25). Another wise saying notes, "Do not withhold good from those who deserve it, when it is in your power to act" (Proverbs 3:27). We always have the power to offer an encouraging word. May we never withhold such a valuable treasure from those traveling down the road of faith with us. Mother Teresa said, "Kind words are easy to speak, but their echoes are truly endless."

The prophet Elisha met a woman who understood that God's people need encouragement along their journey. One day as he was passing through the town of Shunem, a wealthy woman urged him to join her and her husband for dinner. During their time together, she discerned that Elisha was a holy man and decided to build a guest room onto their home for him to use when he came through town. She wanted nothing in return… it was just her way of blessing Elisha, of refreshing him, with her words and ways.

Elisha was overwhelmed by her generosity and wanted to give a gift to her in return. But when he offered to speak to the king on her behalf, she assured him that she did not want, need, or expect anything for her kindness. Elisha wouldn't take no for an answer and continued to contemplate the perfect hostess gift.

Gehazi, his servant, came up with a splendid idea...a child. "Well, she has no son and her husband is old," Gehazi remarked. Great idea. Elisha called her to the doorway and announced, "About this time next year you will hold a son in your arms" (2 Kings 4:16). And she did.

I just love to watch people try to "out nice" each other. That's exactly what we see in the story of Elisha and the woman from Shunem. How wonderful it would be if we used our words to try to "out nice" each other among our brothers and sisters in the church.

Paul wrote, "Let us consider and give attentive, continuous care to watching over one another, studying how we may stir (stimulate and incite) to love and helpful deeds and noble activities" (Hebrews 10:24 AMP). This was not a flippant command. Notice the action words: give attentive care, continuous care, watching over, studying how, stimulate, incite. Notice at the beginning of Paul's exhortation that he instructs us to observe and then to speak. Not every person needs the same word of encouragement. We watch, we pray, and then we speak the words that will refresh them most effectively.

Fanny Crosby is a woman who used the power of her words to affect the church. Fanny was born into a humble household in Southeast, New York, in 1823. When she was six weeks old, Fanny received improper medical care and became blind. Later, she attended the New York School for the Blind. In her forties, she began writing gospel songs.

Well-known hymns such as "Blessed Assurance," "All the Way My Savior Leads Me," and "Saved by Grace" were penned by this servant of God who had a great impact on the church with her words set to song. Kenneth W. Osbeck, author of *101 Hymn Stories,* notes the following about the power of Fanny Crosby's words: "Fanny J. Crosby died at the age of ninety-five. Only eternity will disclose the host of individuals who have been won to a saving faith in Jesus

Christ or those whose lives have been spiritually enriched through the texts of her many hymns."4

We may not be able to write a song, but we can give the gift of encouraging words to set someone's heart to singing.

> Encourage one another and build each other up, just as in fact you are doing. Now we ask you, brothers, to respect those who work hard among you, who are over you in the Lord and who admonish you. Hold them in the highest regard in love because of their work. Live in peace with each other. And we urge you, brothers, warn those who are idle, encourage the timid, help the weak, be patient with everyone (1 Thessalonians 5:11-14).

Where Do You Go for Encouragement?

Nestled 50 feet off Highway 17 in Pawley's Island, South Carolina, rests C.J.'s Beach Club. For years Steve and I eyed the clapboard building tucked in the grove of myrtle trees, but it wasn't the sort of place we would tend to visit. One weekend it was just the two of us on a short holiday at the beach, and we were feeling adventurous. Steve turned the car onto the crushed oyster shell parking lot of C.J.'s, and we decided to taste the local nightlife of the coastal South.

C.J.'s was a dance club. Now, before you close the book in shock that we would darken the doors of such a place, I want you to stay with me a moment. We grew up doing a dance called "The Shag," which is like an East Coast swing. This was shag night at C.J.'s, and the disc jockey spinning the 45s was about 60 years old and had a striking resemblance to my mother-in-law.

Steve and I felt a bit uncomfortable as we walked through the doors and noted the neon signs advertising various drinks, but we were committed. All eyes turned toward the new couple as we walked across the threshold...there was no turning back. The smell of popcorn laced with cigarette smoke filled the air as middle-aged couples shuffled their feet to old beach music under the spinning disco ball.

We each ordered a Coke and found a seat. It wasn't two minutes before a couple wandered over to our table and sat down.

"Hi, I'm Tom," the fortysomething man said as he extended his hand to Steve. "And this is my wife, Julie."

"Hi," Julie chimed in.

"Hi, Julie. Hi, Tom," we returned.

"We've never seen you here before," Tom continued. "Do you live around here?"

"No, we're from Charlotte. Just down here on vacation," Steve answered. "What about you two? Are you from around here?"

"We live in Georgetown just down the road," Tom replied. "We come up here to shag on Friday nights. Most of the people in here are regulars. We all know each other. Like one big family."

After 20 minutes of conversation, we knew each other's occupations, children's ages, college alma mater, favorite hobbies, and various branches of their family tree.

"See you on the dance floor," Tom called as they said their good-byes and made their way to the next table to visit. As soon as they walked away, another couple sat down and the same friendly banter ensued. Then another couple...then another. By the time we left C.J.'s, we felt as though we had been welcomed into the family. We had walked in wary strangers and walked away warm friends.

"Ya'll come back when you're down this way again," several called out as we made our way to the door.

As we drove away in silence with the sound of seashells crunching under our tires, sadness washed over me. "I have been in many churches in my time, but never one that was as welcoming and warm as those folks were tonight," I whispered. "We have a lot to learn." Steve felt the same.

No one said to the people in the dance club, "Now turn and greet someone around you." It was simply spontaneous genuine interest. What is going to attract the world to the church and ultimately a relationship with Jesus Christ? Genuine interest, caring, and concern. More than a tract, door-to-door canvassing, modern facilities, or the latest media-savvy services—potential relationships are the net that brings in a bounty of souls. Like parched cracked ground opening wide for a drop of rain, men and women are longing for their need to love and be loved to be quenched. Will their thirst be satisfied by those of us who have the Living Water in our midst, or will they seek respite elsewhere in a mere mirage of satisfaction? Jesus has what people are truly longing for. Many can't define the longing or who put it there. We know—and we have the privilege of telling them! That's the power of a woman's words.

The Power of a Woman's Words to the World

*The gospel does not fall from the clouds like rain, by accident,
but is brought by the hands of men to where God has sent it.*

—JOHN CALVIN

ONE COLD EVENING during the Christmas season, a little boy was standing out in front of a store window. The little child had no shoes and his clothes were mere rags. A young woman passing by saw the little boy and could read the longing in his pale blue eyes. She took the child by the hand and led him into the store. There she bought him some new shoes and a complete suit of warm clothing.

They came back outside into the street and the woman said to the child, "Now you can go home and have a very happy holiday."

The little boy looked up at her and asked, "Are you God, ma'am?"

She smiled down at him and replied, "No, son. I'm just one of His children."

The little boy then said, "I knew you had to be some relation."[1]

Divine Appointments

As we go throughout our busy days, we are continually met with opportunities to impact others with the words we speak. Yes, our words influence family, friends, and fellow believers. But it is the man in front of us in line at the grocery store, the woman at the checkout counter, the waiter in the restaurant, the fellow passenger on the airplane, the neighbor across the street who might be your special assignment for the day. Those are the people God brings across our paths who may need a word of encouragement most of all.

Jesus was a very busy man. And yet He was never too busy to offer a kind word to the men and women who crossed His path on a daily basis. He stopped and spoke to the diminutive Zacchaeus perched in a tree to get a better look at the parade of followers. He took a break from His travels to engage in one of His longest recorded conversations with a weary woman at a well with a sullied reputation. He interrupted His schedule to comfort a mother in the funeral procession of her only son. He took time to deliver a demon-possessed man who stood in His way on the shore. He noticed a lame man among many who crowded around the pools of Bethesda waiting for the healing waters to stir. He encouraged the distraught Peter after his denial. He comforted His crying mother as she stood at the foot of the cross. He instructed the frustrated fisherman as He stood watching from the shore.

Jesus noticed...and then He offered words and deeds of comfort and concern.

It appears that each of these incidents in Jesus' life was an interruption in His packed schedule, but they were not interruptions at all. Each encounter was a divine appointment from His heavenly Father, who controlled the moments of Jesus' days. Could it be that God is sending us out on special assignment each time we cross the thresholds of our homes? I believe so.

A Universal Need

Advertisers are well aware of the need human beings have to belong. They are banking on it. How many times have my eyes filled with tears over a television commercial? A credit card commercial shows a grown daughter taking her elderly mother back to Italy to discover her roots…"The cost? Priceless." (I cry.) A horse-drawn carriage glides through the snow on its way to a cozy cottage nestled in the trees with smoke swirling in the sky…"Home for the holidays." (I cry.) A young man dressed in a military uniform drops his duffle bag on his unknowing parents' den floor in the wee hours of the morning and starts the coffeemaker. His mother, smelling the aroma, hurries down the stairs and clutches her hands as tears stream down her cheeks at the sight of her soldier home from war. (I cry.)

The tears that form in my eyes prove that these advertisers have tapped into my need to belong. They would have us believe that if we buy their particular product, we will have that warm fuzzy feeling of euphoria or ecstatic joy.

But we know the truth. True joy will not be found on the grocery store shelf, the car sales lot, or the department store window. It cannot be bought with the swipe of a credit card or cold hard cash. People want to feel they are a part of something bigger than themselves and that there is more to this life than accumulated wealth and accomplishments.

We have the power…in our words…to tell the world about the way, the truth, and the life. We have the power…in our words…to help change the world one person at a time.

Simple Words

Alan Loy McGinnis, in his book *The Friendship Factor,* tells this story about the power of a woman's words to one of his friends, Bruce Larson. Bruce was on his way from New Jersey to New York to speak at a conference. He was exhausted and totally unprepared for the schedule before him, but he planned on working during the flight. He opened his notebook and prayed, "O God, help me. Let me get something down here that will be useful to Your people in Syracuse."

Nothing came to Bruce, and the closer he got to Syracuse, the guiltier he felt about his lack of preparation. But then something happened that changed his attitude. It was the simple words of a flight attendant. Bruce remembers:

> About halfway through the brief flight, a stewardess came down the aisle passing out coffee...As she approached my seat, I heard her exclaim, "Hey! Someone is wearing English Leather aftershave lotion...Who is it?"
>
> Eagerly I waved my hand and announced, "It's me."
>
> The stewardess immediately came over and sniffed my cheek, while I sat basking in this sudden attention and appreciating the covetous glances from passengers nearby.
>
> All through the remainder of the flight the stewardess and I maintained a cheerful banter each time she passed my seat...Twenty-five minutes later when the plane prepared to land I realized that my temporary insanity had vanished. Despite the fact that I had failed in every way—in budgeting my time, in preparation, in attitude—everything had changed. I was freshly aware that I loved God and that He loved me in spite of my failure.
>
> What is more, I loved myself and the people around me and the people who were waiting for me in Syracuse...I looked down at the notebook in my lap and found a page full of ideas that could prove useful throughout the weekend.
>
> "God," I mused, "how did this happen?" It was then that I realized that someone had entered my life and turned a key. It was just a small key, turned by a very unlikely person. But the simple act of affirmation, that undeserved and unexpected attention, had got me back into the stream.[2]

This is the power of a woman's words.

Proper Preparation

All through the Bible we have accounts of God sending men and women out into the world with a message. Whether it is a message of repentance, judgment, deliverance, or hope, God made sure the messengers were placed in strategic moments in time to make an impact on those around them. But God doesn't send the messenger out unprepared. He trains them as only He can do.

Let's look at two messengers and how God prepared them to impact the world: Isaiah and Jeremiah.

Isaiah was called to prophesy to Jerusalem 740 years before Christ. In the first five chapters, the overriding theme is impending judgment. "Woe to you who add house to house and join field to field...Woe to those who rise early in the morning to run after their drinks...Woe to those who draw sin along with cords of deceit and wickedness as with cart ropes...Woe to those who call evil good and good evil...Woe to those who are wise in their own eyes and clever in their own sight...Woe to those who are heroes at drinking wine, and champions at mixing drinks..." (Isaiah 5:8,11,18,20-22). But then something happens to Isaiah as he sees his own life reflected in God's magnificent glory.

Isaiah had a vision.

> I saw the Lord seated on a throne, high and exalted, and the train of his robe filled the temple. Above him were seraphs, each with six wings: With two wings they covered their faces, with two they covered their feet, and with two they were flying. And they were calling to one another: "Holy, holy, holy is the LORD Almighty; the whole earth is full of his glory." At the sound of their voices the doorposts and threshold shook and the temple was filled with smoke. "Woe to me!" I cried. "I am ruined! For I am a man of unclean lips, and I live among a people of unclean lips, and my eyes have seen the King, the LORD Almighty" (Isaiah 6:1-5).

I imagine Isaiah was feeling pretty good about himself, being called by God to prophesy to this irksome people. But just when he got out the sixth woe, God decided to hold up the mirror of His holiness in which Isaiah saw his own sin. And where did the sin manifest itself? His words.

God doesn't convict us of our sin to condemn us. He reveals our sin to bring us to repentance and change. Just as Isaiah was lamenting his foul tongue, one of the seraphs (brightly shimmering heavenly beings whose name means "burning ones") picked up a live coal with tongs from the altar of atonement and touched it to the prophet's lips. Just as God sent the Holy Spirit to the believers at Pentecost in the form of flaming tongues, He sent a coal to set Isaiah's tongue afire with cleansing power. The heavenly being touched Isaiah's tongue with the burning coal and then announced that his guilt was taken away.

Now Isaiah was ready to go out into the world and proclaim God's message to His people, and his "Woe is me" was transformed into "Here am I. Send me!" (Isaiah 6:8).

Isaiah didn't need to change his eating or drinking habits. He didn't need to alter his outward appearance or take extra classes at the local seminary. He needed to have his words purified and fortified so God could be properly glorified.

Unlike Isaiah, Jeremiah didn't begin prophesying until God touched his mouth first. Like Isaiah, Jeremiah was called to be a prophet to the Hebrew nation. However, he was very reluctant to heed the call. "I do not know how to speak; I am only a child," he argued. But God reprimanded Jeremiah. "Do not say, 'I am only a child'…Do not be afraid of them, for I am with you and will rescue you."

Then God reached out His hand and touched Jeremiah's mouth and said, "Now, I have put my words in your mouth." God called this young man to be strong and courageous and assured him that He would be with him wherever he went. (To read more about the account, see Jeremiah 1:6-9.)

Now, why did I share these two stories with you? Neither is about a woman or her words. But if God thought it necessary to deal with these two fellows' tongues before they embarked on their heavenly assignment, then we should not think it would be any different for you and for me. But did you notice, in both of these cases, that God initiated the cleansing? It takes more than washing our mouths out with soap to be a woman of clean lips. It takes the power of the Holy Spirit and the touch of God. Our part is to cooperate with Him, submit our words to Him, fill our lives with Him, and live our lives through Him.

Silent Longings

Everyone wants to be noticed, cared for, and loved. How my heart breaks with David's words, "No one cares for my soul" (Psalm 142:4 NKJV). He is crying out during one of the darkest times in his life and felt all alone in his struggle to survive. We might expect to hear those words from the crowded city streets as men and women scurry about in their power suits off to make the next deal. We wouldn't be surprised to hear those words from a vagrant huddled under a bridge with all his worldly possessions stuffed in a plastic grocery bag. But would we expect it from the person sitting beside us in the church pew, the coworker in the next cubicle, or the mother of three next door?

While flying from the East Coast to the West Coast, I watched an in-flight movie, a cleaned-up version of *What Women Want* starring Mel Gibson. Nick Marshall (played by Mel Gibson) works at an advertising firm with a host of busy men and women bustling about in their own little self-absorbed worlds. In a strange twist of events, Nick is "electrically altered" when he slips in the bathroom and falls into the bathtub, along with a hair dryer. When he regains consciousness after his shocking experience, he has the ability to hear women's thoughts. With his new perceptive powers, he lands a huge Nike advertising account and wins the heart of the leading lady...of course. But there is one poignant sideline of the plot that grabbed my heart.

In the movie, one young nondescript woman in Nick's office

has thoughts that stopped Nick in his tracks. *What if I just jumped out the window? Would anyone notice? I could be gone for days and no one would notice...until the files started piling up. Then they'd say, "Where's the geek with the glasses who carries the files?"*

No one noticed the errand girl who refused to make eye contact with her fellow employees...except Nick, who could hear her thoughts.

One day the young woman (who we learn is named Erin), doesn't show up for work.

"Where's Erin?" Nick asked as he notices a pile of files sitting on her desk.

"I don't know," someone replies. "She didn't show up for work today."

Fearing the worst, Nick locates Erin's address and dashes out to stop her from ending her life.

Bursting into her apartment, Nick sees a suicide letter lying on the table and his heart sinks. A startled Erin walks into the room.

"Mr. Marshall, what are you doing here?"

"I'm glad I got here before you hurt yourself."

"What makes you think I was going to hurt myself?"

"I just sensed it."

"Really? You sensed it? That's not good."

Then Nick brilliantly changes course. "The real reason I'm here is to offer you a job. You know we got the Nike account, and we were wondering who would be a real spitfire to work on this project..." Nick offers Erin a place on his team and rescues her from the despair of feeling unwanted, unloved, and unimportant.

I'm not suggesting you watch this movie. After all, it was a cleaned-up airline version. However, I am suggesting that you ponder the situation. I believe men and women walk past us every day, just like Erin in this movie, who feel that they have no significant purpose in this world. Like Erin, I know there are many who feel that their sudden disappearance would cause little fanfare or concern. It might be the woman who passes you in the hall at work, the rebellious-looking teen who shuffles by you at the mall, or the busi-nessman dashing to his next appointment. It takes so little to let someone know they are significant. We have the ability to give someone hope by offering a simple word of acknowledgment.

Dr. David Jeremiah wrote, "We are shaped by those who love us or refuse to love us, and by those whom we love or refuse to love."[3] An amazing opportu-nity is given to each of us as we walk through our day to shape and mold those around us with a simple word of encouragement, acknowledgement, or apprecia-tion. The world is crying out for love—a positive word, a tender touch, a morsel of praise. Some-times a simple "hello" can be a boost to someone starving to be noticed. Many people are so lonely that any token of attention is like a drop of rain on dry parched ground.

So live that you wouldn't be ashamed to sell the family parrot to the town gossip.

—Will Rogers

In *The Four Loves,* C.S. Lewis said, "Our whole being by its very nature is one vast need; incomplete, preparatory, empty yet cluttered, crying out for Him who can untie things that are now knotted together and tie up things that are still dangling loose." How amazing that sometimes God allows us to participate in setting free and binding together through the words we speak.

How do we sprinkle drops of hope onto the desert of a person's soul? It may begin with a smile, a kind word, a simple act of rec-ognition. The realization that each person is uniquely formed in the image of God is an incredible motivation to dispense hope in a desperate world.

As we all know, some people are easier to love than others. But you know what helps me get past the irritating personality, the caustic attitude, or the boorish behavior? Just a little bit of memory. When I reflect back over my past and see just how far God has brought me, I am overwhelmed with gratitude. I don't have to imagine what I would have become if Jesus had not rescued me at the age of 14. I was on the brink of some immoral decisions that would have scarred me for the rest of my life. It was only through His grace and mercy that I did not become a statistic. In *The Brothers Karamazov*, Fyodor Dostoyevsky said, "To truly love someone is to see them as God intended."

Loving LeAnn

Each Christmas my family looks for someone to give a special gift to—usually one that involves giving a portion of ourselves rather than a box with a bow on top. It was not surprising when they quickly agreed with me to make LeAnn and her son our "Christmas Family." She is one of the most caring, loving, and giving people I know. If she had two cents, she would give one away. While she struggled just to keep a roof over her head and food in the fridge, she gathered food and clothing for a young mother in her church and acted as a surrogate mother to a 12-year-old girl who had very little parental care.

LeAnn's husband passed away when her son was two years old. Not having a man around the house left repairs and maintenance issues that she could not handle on her own. So one Christmas Steve and Steven tackled the honey-do list with joy! They loved her! It was a delight!

It was not surprising that Steve and Steven cared for and respected LeAnn. What was surprising is that they had never met her. They formed their opinion strictly on what I had told them about her.

There are many people in the world who will form an opinion about God according to what we say about Him and how we live our lives. We are the first Bible that many people will ever read. What will they think?

Putting the Saints into Circulation

Oliver Cromwell was a political and military leader in Great Britain in the mid-1600s. During his reign, the government began to run low on silver for coins. He sent his men to the local cathedral to see if they could find any precious metals. They reported back.

"The only silver we could find is in the statues of the saints standing in the corners."

Cromwell replied, "Good! We'll melt them down and put them into circulation!"[4]

What a splendid idea! Put the saints in circulation! Paul, when writing to the churches, often referred to Christians as "saints." How fitting that we be melted down and put into circulation, dispensing encouraging words like treasured coins into the heart pockets of a hurting world.

I am convinced that a buffet of ministry exists in restaurants. If ever there was a place where the saints are put into circulation, it is at eating establishments. Americans are eating out now more than at any other time in our country's history, so let's take a look at this mission field being served up every day. Here are three scenarios to ponder.

Scenario One

The waiter was haughty, harried, and hurried. Our very presence seemed to be an inconvenience to his evening. His body language shouted, "What do you want? I'm in a hurry. Be quick about it. I don't like you and I don't want to be here." So I decided to try a little experiment.

"You sure are busy tonight," I said as he plopped our drinks on the table.

"Yep."

"I bet you're going to sleep well tonight."

"Yep."

"I've been watching you scurry around from table to table. You're doing a great job."

Then the waiter looked me in the eye for the first time, stood a bit straighter, and unwrinkled his brow.

When he returned to the table, I continued my experiment. "How long have you been working here?" I asked.

"About four months," he replied. "I had been working in the corporate world and needed to get off the treadmill...the rat race. This is a different type of pressure, but I've lost thirty pounds and feel better than I've felt in years. I'm thinking about going to culinary school in the fall."

"That sounds like a wonderful idea," I said. "I bet you'd be great at it."

He smiled and turned away. Someone noticed that he was more than a waiter...he was a person.

The waiter who gave us our tab at the end of the meal was not the same man who had taken our order an hour before. He had on the same clothes, wore the same name tag, and served the same station. But the frustrated, cold waiter who sloshed our iced tea on the table had warmed into a cheerful young man. That's the power of a woman's words.

Scenario Two

The restaurant was bustling with activity. We bowed our heads to pray as the uncomfortable waitress stood to the side holding a basket of bread. We said our "amens," and then she politely placed the basket on the table and scurried away.

It didn't take long before one of the women in our group began to complain. I knew her propensity to grumble and held my breath. The rolls were cold, the meat was tough, the knife had a spot on it, and where was the ketchup anyway! Several times she pestered the waitress with her nitpicky criticism. I wished we had not prayed. I didn't want anyone observing this woman's critical spirit to know we were representatives of Jesus Christ.

We can all do Jesus a favor. The next time we go out to eat, whether it is at McDonald's or Morton's of Chicago, let's represent Jesus well. We can use our words to make those around us hungry and thirsty to know the hope that is within us. May our compliments flow and grateful spirits nurture their souls.

Scenario Three

I called our waitress over to our table. "Excuse me," I began. "Could I please see the manager?"

"Of course," she nervously replied.

In a few moments, the manager came over to the table. "Is there a problem?" he asked.

"Not at all," I answered. "I just wanted to tell you what a marvelous job Missy did taking care of us today. She is a wonderful waitress, and I hope we have the pleasure of having her wait on us again next time. I just thought you should know what a great job she did and what a treasure you have."

"Thank you, ma'am."

Missy came back to the table beaming. No doubt the manager had relayed our praise. It only took a minute, and those words meant much more to Missy than a 20 percent tip.

> *I'm just a nobody telling everybody about somebody who can save anybody.*
>
> —Author Unknown

Now, let's chew on these three scenarios and digest the ramifications of each. At which table do you see yourself? At which table would you like to join?

God's Living Letters

I received a letter the other day. It didn't have a stamp in the right-hand corner or even a return address sticker, but I knew exactly where it came from, and there was no doubt as to who had sent it.

The letter was wearing jeans and a sweatshirt with brown shoulder-length hair, and she was sent by God.

In the Bible, Paul described Christians as living letters known and read by everybody, not written with ink, but with the Spirit of God on human hearts (2 Corinthians 3:2-3). God has sent many love letters my way…hand delivered, special delivery, postage paid. Admittedly, some of the letters seem to have become marred in transit, and I suspect a few of the words were not quite what the Author intended. But they were letters nonetheless.

God did not write His letters on fragile sheets of paper or on tablets of stone. He wrote His letters on human hearts for all the world to read. There are some letters that I've received and wanted to mark RETURN TO SENDER across the top. I didn't want the letter and, honestly, I wasn't sure where it came from. It couldn't possibly be from God. The words were harsh, and I suspected they were also counterfeit. Not really from God at all…even though the letter said they were.

Then there are other letters I have received that were so beautifully scripted that I take them out and read them over and over again. They are treasures I hold dear. I read them often, clutch them to my heart, and even place a kiss upon the seal from time to time. These are my favorite letters. They come in all shapes and sizes, but the return address is always evident, even if it has faded with years or rubbed off with wear. I love these letters. God has sent me so many over the years.

Dear friend, here is a daunting thought. You are a letter. I am a letter. God has written His message on our hearts and mailed us out to the world. People read His letters in our actions. They read His letters in our words. What will they read in your letter? Will they welcome the words like a soldier hungry for news from home, or view them like junk mail to be tossed in the trash? Will they dread the words and see them like a bill that needs to be paid, or will they see them as God intended…loving words wooing them to Christ?

The World's Guest Book

Just before leaving our rented condominium after a week of sun, sand, and surf at Hilton Head Island, South Carolina, we found a treasure tucked under some old magazines on the coffee table. It was a small white guest book, signed by previous vacationers who had also shared a relaxing week away from home.

Feeling somewhat like a Peeping Tom craning to peer into someone's window, we cracked open the book and stole a glimpse into the personalities of our fellow travelers. With each entry we visualized what the guests looked like, decided if we would like to invite them over for dinner, and surmised whether they had an enjoyable vacation together.

Have a look for yourself and decide with whom you would like to share a cup of coffee or would like to have as your neighbor:

- "Thank you very much for the use of your condo. We thoroughly enjoyed our first but not last visit to SC."

- "Had a great time. Enjoyed your villa very much! However, you need to have the springs in the couch repaired. Very uncomfortable to sit on. Thank you."

- "We have decided that this is where we'd love to live. It's a golfer's dream. Your courses are beautiful. The girls loved the beach, parasailing, bike rides, horseback riding, shopping! I love my tan. We will be back to visit! If you are ever in Arkansas, come to Stuttgart. We are 50 miles east of Little Rock. Stuttgart hosts the World Championship Duck Calling Contest every year during Thanksgiving weekend. We are known as the "Rice and Duck Capital of the World." Riceland Rice comes from our little town, and the ducks feed off the rice fields during the winter after harvest. It is some of the best duck hunting anywhere. Thank you for the use of your condo. We've had a great week here."

- "We really enjoyed your villa, but we won't be staying here again. We just booked another villa at Colonnade for next year a couple of doors down for almost $300 less."

- "Hello. My name is Katie and I got here yesterday. So far we are having a good time. I'm eleven years old and I came here with my mother, grandmother, and my Aunt Barbara. She got here at the same time we did, but she is leaving tomorrow. We came all the way from Lake Wylie, SC. I love it here and might be back next year."

- "It has been a fabulous time. This villa is bigger than our home! My niece is sure she saw a whale at the Old Oyster Factory, but we are sure she saw a buoy. Nick and Dad played golf together and we all played mini-golf. We went bike riding and 'gator chasing.' The ocean is breathtaking. I've never seen it before, so I'm still in awe!"

- "When we first came, the keys wouldn't fit, you forgot to give us a pass, and we almost ran over a biker. Get better service! Two grandmas were with us! Sixth time here—never happened before."

The Bible tells us that we are simply visitors here on earth (1 Chronicles 29:15), and our words, while they are letters from God, are also entries in the Guest Book of Life. What entries am I writing with my attitudes, actions, and words for all the world to see? Will they think that I was a crabby old lady who wanted better service? Will they think I savored each day here with my wonderful family? Will they think that I would have preferred another life just a few doors down? Or will they think that I so enjoyed my time here that I wanted to share it with anyone and everyone who was passing through?

Lost and Found

Once there was a little girl who grew up in a very nice neighborhood with 60-foot pine trees that shaded a Southern ranch-style home. Her life consisted of a smattering of friends who roamed from house to house, barefoot hot summer days, and a collie named Lassie who followed her every move. But behind the doors of her house was a family secret. Her father, a businessman in the community, had a drinking problem. Many nights this little girl climbed in bed to the sound of her parents yelling, fighting, and crashing furniture. No one knew what was happening behind the beautiful brick walls and manicured lawn.

But there was a woman in her neighborhood, the mother of this little girl's best friend. She loved this little girl and shared Jesus Christ with her. She listened to her troubles, embraced her in her arms, and made her feel as though she was extremely loved by God. Their relationship, this bond between a lost little girl and a borrowed mom, continued to grow. Then one day, Mrs. Henderson asked this 14-year-old teen if she was ready to accept Jesus Christ as her Lord and Savior.

"Are you ready to make Jesus Lord of your life?" she asked.

The little girl said yes.

The little girl was me.

I am the product of the power of a woman's words. Mrs. Henderson's words to me about Jesus Christ and God's love changed my life. But it wasn't just her words about Jesus that made the difference. It was her words about life in general that drew me like iron shavings to a magnet. She made me want what she had—excitement, enthusiasm, and a zest for life.

Most people are not drawn to Jesus because of an advertising campaign, a sign along the road, or a steeple along the skyline. Most people are drawn to Christ through cords of kindness formed in relationships with other people.

We have the power in our words to make people thirsty to know Christ. It doesn't necessarily come through preaching. It comes through loving, listening, and learning. "How, then, can they call on the one they have not believed in? And how can they believe in the one of whom they have not heard? And how can they hear without someone preaching to them? And how can they preach unless they are sent? As it is written, 'How beautiful are the feet of those who bring good news!'" (Romans 10:14-15). That is the power of a woman's words to the world.

Simple Words of Kindness

- Compliment service workers.

- Show interest and concern when someone appears to be having a bad day.

- Say thank you.

- Ask questions about someone's interests. "I see you are buying a wedding present. Is it for someone close to you?"

- Greet your neighbors.

- Learn your neighbors' names and write them encouraging notes during difficult times.

- Find something positive to say to the cashier at the checkout line.

- Start a conversation with the person beside you on a bus, in an airplane, or in line at the post office.

- Offer to help someone. For example, you see a woman struggling with her packages and the baby stroller all at the same time. A simple, "Here, let me help you with that," could be just the words to brighten her day.

- When you see an embarrassed young mother with a child acting up, encourage her with kind words such as, "You're doing a great job" or "Mine did the same thing when he was little."

- Speak kindly to the kids in the neighborhood. So many adults talk down to kids; they'll think you're the greatest!

THE POWER OF A WOMAN'S WORDS TO GOD

*Prayer is the conduit through which power
from heaven is brought to earth.*

—O. HALLESBY

TO BETH IT WAS the confusion of an inept airline. To me, it was a divine appointment from God.

"Someone's in my seat," the disheveled young woman complained as she stumbled into the airplane.

"This one is empty," I pointed out.

"Thanks," she huffed as she plopped down beside me.

The beautiful young lady was obviously exhausted. She was dressed in skintight jeans and a distracting low-cut T-shirt. Her flip-flops slid under her feet to reveal a tattoo on the top of her right foot. Sunglasses hid something...I wasn't sure what. She looked straight ahead, but I felt that her mind was traveling to a distant place.

After the plane left the ground, I pulled out my latest book that I was reviewing for an upcoming radio interview. *Put the book down and talk to this girl,* God seemed to say.

Lord, she doesn't want to talk. I can tell by her body language. She's not interested in conversation, I mentally argued.

Put the book down and talk to this girl. (God can be very persistent. Especially when it comes to one of His little lost lambs.)

I closed the book and turned to this...kid.

"So where are you headed?" I asked.

"Home," she replied.

"Where's home?"

"Right outside of Charlotte," she replied. "It's a small town. I'm sure you've never heard of it."

"Were you in Florida on business or pleasure?" I continued.

"I was visiting my boyfriend," she answered.

Then she took off her sunglasses to reveal red swollen eyes. She glanced down at the book in my lap. *"Your Scars Are Beautiful to God,"* she read out loud. "That's an interesting topic. I've got lots of scars."

"So do I. That's why I wrote the book."

"You wrote that book?"

"Yep."

> The effective, fervent prayer of a righteous man [wife, mother, friend] avails much.
>
> —JAMES 5:16 NKJV

For the next hour and a half, she poured out her heart. She had been abandoned by her birth father and sexually abused by several men in her life. She was on this flight home because her boyfriend, who had just come out of a drug rehabilitation center, had roughed her up. Actually, she was fleeing. My heart broke as this beautiful young girl told me story after story of cruelties that had been done *to* her mingled with bad choices that had been made *through* her. At the moment her life resembled a hundred-car train wreck with one lone survivor who was in desperate need of resuscitation.

As my mind engaged with Beth (not her real name), my spirit communed with God. *What do I do?* I prayed. *So much hurt. So much pain.*

Pray for her...now.

"Beth, would you mind if I prayed for you?"

"No," she said with a quiver in her voice. "I'd like that."

I held Beth's hand and God's sorrow for this girl filled my heart. It wasn't just a "God bless Beth" sort of prayer. I sobbed. It was as if God's pain for this girl I didn't even know was flowing through me.

As God would have it, Beth and I were on the front row of a sparsely filled plane. The only person paying any attention to us was the flight attendant, who sat facing us in her jump seat. I'm not sure, but I think God was working in her heart as well.

When the plane landed, I handed Beth the book, we exchanged e-mails, and we embraced one last time. Since then we have kept in touch, and Beth has continued her journey for peace and purpose. Her stepfather wrote me a letter expressing his appreciation for taking the time to minister to his "little girl." He wrote: "I had been praying for God to send Beth an angel, and I believe He did."

Well, I'm no angel, that's for sure. But I believe the angels were hovering around us in that plane. The airplane may have been soaring in the sky, but Beth and I flew to the throne room of God.

One of the great mysteries of the Christian life is that God has given us great power through prayer. Through the pages of the Bible and the volumes of history, we see God mightily working on behalf of those who seek Him in prayer. There is great power in the words of a woman offered up to God. However, unlike the power of our words to our children, our husbands, our friends, the church, and the world, this power comes from God. He simply invites us to open the floodgates of heaven with our words.

All through our lives there will be times when we feel powerless. But, friend, we are never *more* power*ful* than when we use our words in prayer. I was only with Beth a few hours in that airplane, but God's power was evident when we grasped hands and prayed. His transforming power did more in a few moments than any human could have done in years.

Hannah's Powerful Prayer

Hannah was a desperate woman. She had a wonderful husband and a comfortable home, but she didn't have what she wanted most... a child. She longed to feel the movement of a babe in her womb, nestle an infant in the crook of her arm, and suckle a child at her breast. But her empty arms served as a constant reminder of a barren womb and a hollow heart.

Her husband's very name, Elkanah, meant "God has created [a son]"[1] and yet she could not give him a namesake. Elkanah didn't understand Hannah's pain. "Hannah, why are you weeping? Why don't you eat? Why are you downhearted? Don't I mean more to you than ten sons?" (1 Samuel 1:8).

In those days, it was customary for a man to take a second wife if his first wife proved to be barren. Polygamy entered history when haughty Lamech, the seventh generation from Adam in the line of Cain, sought to increase his power and prestige by marrying two women to produce more children (Genesis 4:19). Although polygamy was never God's intention, it became a common practice. So Elkanah chose Peninnah for his second wife, and she proved to be very fertile indeed.

I cannot imagine living in a house with two wives. There is an old saying, "Too many cooks in the kitchen spoil the broth." Well, friend, too many wives in the bedroom spoil a lot more than dinner!

Peninnah was a jealous, vindictive woman. She used her prolific childbearing ability to needle Hannah constantly. She knew Hannah was Elkanah's favorite wife and that she was more or less his brood mare. Yes, she might have given him children, but she knew...yes, she knew that she did not possess his heart. Day and night Peninnah used her words to taunt Hannah. "Too bad you don't have any children to tuck in bed at night," she might have said. "What good is a cow with no milk or a chicken with no eggs," she might have whispered. "Fit only for the butcher, I'd say."

The Bible says: "[Hannah's] rival kept provoking her in order to irritate her. This went on year after year" (1 Samuel 1:6-7). Did you catch that? It wasn't simply "day after day," but rather "year after year." Long-term, chronic contention.

Elkanah tried his best to make up for Hannah's emptiness. Three times a year, when the family traveled to worship at the temple in Shiloh, Elkanah gave portions of meat to Peninnah and to all her sons and daughters. But to Hannah he gave a double portion. Elkanah's kindness only stirred Peninnah's jealousy and heightened her provocation. Hannah didn't want the extra sacrificial meat. She wanted a child. Elkannah could not fill the emptiness with extra servings of kindness. But Hannah knew the One who could. During one of her travels to the temple, Hannah poured her heart out to God in prayer. Let's pick up the story in 1 Samuel 1:9-20:

> Once when they had finished eating and drinking in Shiloh, Hannah stood up. Now Eli the priest was sitting on a chair by the doorpost of the LORD's temple. In bitterness of soul Hannah wept much and prayed to the LORD. And she made a vow, saying, "O LORD Almighty, if you will only look upon your servant's misery and remember me, and not forget your servant but give her a son, then I will give him to the LORD for all the days of his life, and no razor will ever be used on his head." As she kept on praying to the LORD, Eli observed her mouth. Hannah was praying in her heart, and her lips were moving but her voice was not heard. Eli thought she was drunk and said to her, "How long will you keep on getting drunk? Get rid of your wine." "Not so, my lord," Hannah replied, "I am a woman who is deeply troubled. I have not been drinking wine or beer; I was pouring out my soul to the LORD. Do not take your servant for a wicked woman; I have been praying here out of my great anguish and grief." Eli answered, "Go in peace, and may the God of Israel grant you what you have asked of him." She said, "May your servant find favor in your eyes." Then she went her way and ate something, and her

face was no longer downcast. Early the next morning they arose and worshiped before the LORD and then went back to their home at Ramah. Elkanah lay with Hannah his wife, and the LORD remembered her. So in the course of time Hannah conceived and gave birth to a son. She named him Samuel, saying, "Because I asked the LORD for him."

What strikes me most about Hannah is that she brought her sorrows to God. She did not use her words to retaliate against Peninnah's taunting, but rather gave her pain to God in prayer. She didn't pray proudly as though she *deserved* a child, but humbly, as a servant pleading to her Master. Her anguish was so intense that words formed in her heart and moved her lips, but they did not produce a sound. Like a crying child pausing to gasp for air, the silence of Hannah's prayer pierced God's heart.

> *If any of you lacks wisdom, he should ask God, who gives generously to all without finding fault, and it will be given to him.*
>
> —JAMES 1:5

"The prayer of a righteous person is powerful and effective" (James 5:16 TNIV). God heard Hannah's prayer and acted on her behalf. The Bible says that God "remembered Hannah." That does not mean that He had forgotten her or had not taken note of her in the past. What it does mean is that He was about to act. All through the Bible we read the words "God remembered": "God remembered Noah" (Genesis 8:1), "[God] remembered Abraham" (Genesis 19:29), "God remembered Rachel" (Genesis 30:22). Each time we see those words, we can know that God is about to act on someone's behalf. Be assured of this. God never forgets and He always sees.

We can see the power of a woman's words in prayer in the life of Hannah. Not only did God answer her prayer and give her a son, He made her the mother of one of the greatest prophets in the recorded history of Israel...Samuel. He answered her prayer "exceedingly abundantly" beyond all that she could have asked or imagined (Ephesians 3:20 NKJV).

Monica's Prayer

Reading the story of Hannah reminds me of the story of another woman whose prayers birthed another man who made a great impact on the world...Monica, the mother of Augustine. But rather than physical birth, it was her son's spiritual birth that resulted from her hours of intercession.

Many know of the writings of Augustine and his great impact on the church, but they might not know that without the power of a woman's words in prayer, those pages of history would read very differently. The following is an excerpt from my book *Being a Great Mom, Raising Great Kids:*

> From the time he [Augustine] was born, she [his mother] prayed he would surrender his life to Christ and affect the world for God. However, Augustine's pagan father was just as zealous to lead young Augustine into sin as his mother was to introduce him to Christ.
>
> Augustine himself said that from the time he was born, he was "sealed with Christ's cross." However, he sidestepped God with the determination of a prizefighter.
>
> In his early heathen years, Augustine attended the University of Carthage and received an excellent education in grammar, logic, literature, language, and oratory. During his years of higher education, he also experienced heavy doses of corruption, brothels, and friends in low places.
>
> He graduated into a lifestyle of immorality, alcohol, and sexual promiscuity, living with one woman for 15 years and fathering a child with her. However, they never married. Eventually, he became a Manichean, which would compare to joining a modern day cult.

Even though Augustine was living in apparent destitution of the soul, his mother continued to pray for him…Twice a day…she went to church and cried out to the Lord on Augustine's behalf.

> *Ask and it will be given to you; seek and you will find; knock and the door will be opened to you. For everyone who asks receives; he who seeks finds; and to him who knocks the door will be opened.*
>
> —MATTHEW 7:7-8

One day Monica approached a bishop who was bold in confronting others about their relationship to God and their need for salvation. She begged him to talk to Augustine, but he refused, saying that her son was *unteachable.* Still, as the bishop walked away, he replied, "It cannot be that the son of these tears should perish."

Shortly afterwards, Monica sensed that Augustine was planning to leave Carthage on a ship to Rome. When she confronted him at the dock, he denied it and said that he was only there to bid a friend farewell. However, the next morning, she discovered that her son had lied. He had set sail for Rome and escaped her influence—or so it seemed. What she did not realize was that as her wayward son turned his eyes toward the shores of home, he pictured in his mind's eye that faithful beacon, pointing him to the safety of Christ's harbor and the one true God.

Monica's prayers followed her son to Rome, and God continued to put people in his path to point him to the Savior. One day, while Augustine read one of Paul's letters in the Bible, the Holy Spirit touched his heart and opened his eyes. He knew those letters were written to him, and he committed his life to Jesus Christ.

Augustine went on to write more than one hundred books and one thousand sermons. The *Encyclopedia Britannica* describes him as "the dominant personality of the Western Church of his time…generally recognized as having been the greatest thinker of Christian antiquity." His books *City of God* and *Confessions* are classics still read today. Sixteen hundred years later, the church still reaps the benefits of this praying mother.

Shortly after Augustine became a Christian, his mother said that she felt her work on earth was accomplished. One week later, at the age of fifty-six, she died.

In one of his prayers Augustine wrote the following about his mother, "She poured out her tears and her prayers all the more fervently, begging you [God] to speed your help and give me light in my darkness." Another entry reads, "My mother, your faithful servant, wept to you for me, shedding more tears for my spiritual death than other mothers shed for the bodily death of a son. For in her faith and in the spirit which she had from you she looked down on me as dead. You heard her and did not despise the tears which streamed down and watered the earth in every place where she bowed her head in prayer."[2]

Can we go back to the girl I prayed for on the plane? While I prayed for Beth on the plane, her mother was praying for her at home. For years Beth's mother had been praying for her to turn her life over to Christ. She prayed, just like Monica, that God would put people in her path to point her to the truth of the cross. And that chilly night in October, God answered this mother's prayer.

The Real Battle

Paul was keenly aware of the power of prayer. He wrote these words to the Ephesians:

> Be strong in the Lord and in his mighty power. Put on the full armor of God so that you can take your stand against the devil's schemes. For our struggle is not against flesh and blood, but against the rulers, against the authorities, against the powers of this dark world and against the spiritual forces of evil in the heavenly realms...And pray in the

Spirit on all occasions with all kinds of prayers and requests. With this in mind, be alert and always keep on praying for all the saints (Ephesians 6:10-12,18).

He also wrote about his battle in 2 Corinthians 10:3-4:

Though we live in the world, we do not wage war as the world does. The weapons we fight with are not the weapons of the world. On the contrary, they have divine power to demolish strongholds.

When someone crossed my country grandmother, she used to say, "Them's fightin' words." Well, friend, them's fightin' words. Our words to God have the power of spiritual dynamite to demolish the power of Satan in our lives.

Paul's Request for Prayer

Paul understood the power of our words to God in prayer, and he asked the recipients of his letter to pray for him: "I urge you, brothers, by our Lord Jesus Christ and by the love of the Spirit, to join me in my struggle by praying to God for me" (Romans 15:30). "Pray also for me, that whenever I open my mouth, words may be given me so that I will fearlessly make known the mystery of the gospel, for which I am an ambassador in chains. Pray that I may declare it fearlessly, as I should" (Ephesians 6:19-20).

The New Testament was originally written in Greek, and sometimes looking at the original definitions of the words can give us great insight. The Greek word Paul uses for "struggle" in Romans 15:30 is *sunagonizomai,* which means "to struggle in company of; i.e., to be a partner (assistant), strive together with."[3] The root word means "to endeavor to accomplish something: fight, labor fervently, strive." For example, to compete for a prize or to contend with an adversary.[4]

Prayer for another person is not simply a nice platitude or a pat on the back. When we tell someone we will pray for them, we are agreeing to put on the armor and head to the front lines of battle on their behalf.

Many ancient shields had brackets attached to the sides. These brackets were a type of latch that soldiers could use to lock during battle. When the shields were locked together, the soldiers moved as one force, forming a barricade against the enemy. Alone, the shield was a small defense. Together, they formed a human wall. Do you see the significance? When we lock arms in prayer with others, we are locking our shields together and forming a powerfully strong fortress of defense.

> *Whatever you ask for in prayer, believe that you have received it, and it will be yours.*
>
> —MARK 11:24

One night I was in the restroom touching up my makeup before speaking to several hundred women. I was having one of those moments when I looked in the mirror and my thoughts began to swirl in my mind. *What am I doing here? What do I possibly have to say to these women that could make any difference in their lives? I am not capable of walking to that podium tonight.*

While I was mulling over the lies, the fiery darts that Satan was shooting into my mind, my cell phone rang.

"Hello."

"Hi, Sharon. This is Mary. Where are you?"

"Actually, I'm standing in the restroom at a speaking engagement getting ready to walk out on the stage. I forgot to turn off my cell phone!"

"I want you to know," Mary continued, "that God interrupted me while I was cooking dinner and told me to pray for you. Not only that, He told me to call you now."

I was imagining Mary standing in her kitchen with spaghetti sauce simmering on the stove and stopping mid-stir. There might have been a little conversation with God that went something like this: *Call Sharon and pray for her,* God might have said.

Could You just wait a minute, God? The sauce is almost done.

Call Sharon and pray for her.

Okay, okay, I'll do it now.

There was great power in Mary's instant obedience. If she had waited, I would not have known she was praying. Not only did God prompt her to pray at that moment, He wanted her to tell me she was doing so. Why? God knew there was power in her prayer, and He wanted me to know that I was not going into battle alone. He had called Mary to "struggle with me," to "strive together in battle," to lock arms with me and march into victory.

> *True prayer is when God's heart is expressed through your words.*
>
> —JENNIFER KENNEDY DEAN

Sharon Betters had that same experience with a group of her friends after she had lost her 16-year-old son, Mark, in a car accident. "Shattered by the intrusion of death," she said, "I soon learned why Scripture calls it our enemy (1 Corinthians 15:26). Every day brought reminders of Mark's physical absence—an empty bedroom, an untouched jacket, his dog patiently waiting on the bed, his brothers and sister wailing loudly or quietly weeping."[5]

Many men and women locked shields and surrounded this family with prayer. Her husband experienced firsthand the power of a woman's words in prayer.

Four months after Mark's death, Sharon agreed to give a short devotional at a women's conference about the miracle of the ministry of encouragement. After she spoke, the event coordinator asked the four hundred women in attendance to pray for Sharon's husband, Chuck. When she asked for specific prayer for Chuck, she knew God was using the prayers of these women to meet needs only He could have known. Later that evening, Chuck telephoned Sharon and asked what she was doing between 9:15 and 9:30 that evening. She told him about the women praying specifically for him. When she arrived home, he told her the following story.

> All alone in our home for the first time since Mark's death, I felt overwhelming anguish and longing for our son. I tried to distract myself by reading, studying, and watching basketball. Nothing worked. I begged God to comfort me, but instead of God's nearness, I felt an ominous murky presence in our home. Finally, I gave up trying to stop the pain and turned out all the lights, matching the black night in my soul with physical darkness. Anguish mounted as the demons of doubt and despair attacked. It was 9:15. Then at 9:30, the ominous darkness was gone. The strangling grief melted. Although I still yearned for Mark, the longing was bearable.[6]

Can you just see the women locking shields in prayer for this man? Can you see God roll away the cloud as angels won the war over the demons surrounding his home? Oh, the power of a woman's words in prayer. Consider the words of this poem.

The Warrior

This morning my thoughts traveled along
To a place in my life where days have since gone
Beholding an image of what I used to be
As visions were stirred, and God spoke to me

He showed me a Warrior, a soldier in place
Positioned by Heaven, yet I saw not the face
I watched as the Warrior fought enemies
That came from the darkness with destruction for me

I saw as the Warrior would dry away tears
As all of Heaven's Angels hovered so near
I saw many wounds on the Warrior's face
Yet weapons of warfare were firmly in place

I felt my heart weeping, my eyes held so much
As God let me feel the Warrior's prayer touched
I thought "how familiar" the words that were prayed
The prayers were like lightning that never would fade

I said to God, "Please, the Warrior's name"
He gave no reply, he chose to refrain
I asked, "Lord, who is broken that they need such prayer?"
He showed me an image of myself standing there

Bound by confusion, lost and alone
I felt prayers of the Warrior carry me home
I asked, "Please show me, Lord, this Warrior so true"
I watched and I wept, for Mother...the Warrior—was you!

©1993 LARRY S. CLARK

Billy Sunday once said, "All hell cannot tear a boy or girl away from a praying mother." Whether it is interceding in prayer for our children, husbands, friends, fellow believers, or the world, there is no more powerful way we can use our words than petitioning Almighty God to work on their behalf.

The Power of a Crippled Young Girl

G. Campbell Morgan tells a story about the power of one woman's prayers to stir a revival in her home church.

There are saints of God who for long, long years have been shut off from all the activities of the Church, and even from the worship of the sanctuary, but who, nevertheless, have continued to labor together in prayer with the whole fellowship of the saints. There comes to me the thought of one woman who, to my knowledge, since 1872 in this great babel of London, has been in perpetual pain, and yet in constant prayer. She is today a woman twisted and distorted by suffering, and yet exhaling the calm and strength of the secret of the Most High. In 1872 she was a bed-ridden girl in the North of London, praying that God would send revival to the Church of which she was a member, and yet into which even then she never came. She had read in the little paper called *Revival*, which subsequently became *The Christian*, the story of a work being done in Chicago among ragged children by a man called Moody. She had never seen Moody, but putting that little paper under her pillow, she began to pray, "O Lord, send this man to our Church." She had no means of reaching him or communicating with him. He had already visited the country in 1867, and in 1872 he started again for a short trip with no intention of doing any work. Mr. Lessey, however, the pastor of the church of which this girl was a member, met him and asked him to preach for him. He consented, and after the evening service he asked those who would decide for Christ to rise, and hundreds did so. He was surprised and imagined that his request had been misunderstood. He repeated it more clearly, and again the response was the same. Meetings were continued through the following ten days, and four hundred members were taken into the church. In telling me this story Moody said, "I wanted to know what this meant. I began making inquiries and never rested until I found a bed-ridden girl praying that God would bring me to that Church. He (God) had heard her, and brought me over four thousand miles of land and sea in answer to her request.[7]

One little crippled lamb by the name of Marianne Adlard uttered fervent prayers to Almighty God on behalf of her flock, and God sent a shepherd to gather the sheep from all around England. Amazing... the power of a woman's words to God!

The *Potential* to *Change*

*T*HE *P*ROMISE OF *P*OWER

Before Pentecost the disciples found it hard to do easy things;
after Pentecost they found it easy to do hard things.

—A.J. GORDON

IT WAS A DAUNTING SCENE. More than 1200 miles of Alaskan shore-line was covered with black slimy crude oil, more than 1000 bodies of once bustling sea otters were littering the coast, and more than 100,000 grounded birds were gasping for air. The *Exxon Valdez* oil spill of 1988 dumped 11 million gallons of crude oil into the Prince William Sound and disrupted the ecological balance of nature. Many of its most beautiful inhabitants, including 150 bald eagles, were killed. The once glacier-fed waters teeming with life became an oily death trap.

Just as toxins in nuclear waste facilities, city dumps, and indus-trial accidents wreak havoc on the environment, toxic words cause destruction to the hearts and souls of the people. Paul wrote, "Let no foul or polluting language...[ever] come out of your mouth" (Ephesians 4:29 AMP). Perhaps as you've read the previous chapters you've cringed at words you've spoken and you wish you could take them back. Words that have polluted the ones you hold dear. Can we clean up the mess and repair the damage? Absolutely! We can choose to dismantle the verbal weapons and break the patterns of toxic words.

Relying on the Holy Spirit

Tongues...most animals have one. Some snakes have forked tongues. Lizards smell with their tongues. Some fish, such as salmon and trout, have teeth on their tongues. Frogs and toads have tongues that whip out at incredible speeds to catch flies and other insects. Their cousin, the chameleon, has a tongue that is as long as its body. An anteater's tongue can stretch to the height of a two-year-old. A gecko uses its tongue to wipe across its eyes like a windshield, and a giraffe uses its 20-inch tongue to clean its ears. The tongue of a blue whale is about the size and weight of a full-grown African elephant.

Even though a human tongue cannot smell out dinner, reel in the catch of the day, or reach to the tops of trees to pick fruit, it can do something even more amazing. The human tongue can create words. Words are an incredible gift, and as we have seen, they have the potential for good or evil. How do we harness such energy and ensure that it is only used for good? Unfortunately, James tells us it is impossible.

"All kinds of animals, birds, reptiles and sea creatures are being tamed and have been tamed by human beings, but no one can tame the tongue" (James 3:7 TNIV). That's the bad news. Now, here's the good news. While no human being can tame the tongue...God can. It may be impossible for James, and for you and for me, but it is not impossible for God. "Is anything too hard for the LORD?" God asked Abraham after announcing that Sarah's 90-year-old body was going to bear a child (Genesis 18:14).

When we come to faith in Jesus Christ, God gives us the gift of the Holy Spirit. The Holy Spirit is the third person of the Trinity who enables us to do all that God has called us to do. He gives us the power to change!

Jesus explained to the disciples: "You will receive power when the Holy Spirit comes on you; and you will be my witnesses in

Jerusalem, and in all Judea and Samaria, and to the ends of the earth" (Acts 1:8). After Jesus' ascension into heaven, the disciples waited for the Holy Spirit as Jesus had instructed.

> When the day of Pentecost came, they were all together in one place. Suddenly, a sound like the blowing of a violent wind came from heaven and filled the whole house where they were sitting. They saw what seemed to be tongues of fire that separated and came to rest on each of them. All of them were filled with the Holy Spirit and began to speak in other tongues as the Spirit enabled them (Acts 2:1-4).

Isn't it interesting that the first manifestation of the power of the Holy Spirit was words and the first visual manifestation was tongues of fire? The disciples were able to speak in the various languages of the men and women who were visiting Jerusalem to celebrate Pentecost. The travelers heard the gospel in their own languages! Yes, that was astonishing. But even more amazing was the courage that arose in the cowardly disciples.

Just a short time before Pentecost, Peter had been so afraid that he denied he even knew who Jesus was. A mere servant girl's question had Peter shaking in his sandaled feet and swearing he was no friend of Jesus. But after being filled with the Holy Spirit, Peter stood up, raised his voice, and addressed the crowd with such a mighty sermon that 3000 men and women accepted Jesus as their Savior and were baptized. That's what the Holy Spirit can do for timid souls who believe. He can transform a cursing tongue into a confessing tongue.

It is only through the power of the Holy Spirit that we are able to control this little muscle that rests between our teeth. However, change does require our cooperation. We must work in tandem with the Holy Spirit to rein in this feisty force. The Holy Spirit gives us the power, but our responsibility is to put God-given principles into practice.

Holocaust survivor Corrie ten Boom spent the last years of her life speaking to men and women all around the world about the God who sustained her during her imprisonment and who delivered her from the Nazi prison camps. During one of her presentations, she held up a lady's white glove.

"What can this white glove do?" she asked. Then she went on to explain…

> The glove can do nothing. "Oh, but if my hand is in the glove, it can do many things…cook, play the piano, write. Well, you say that is not the glove but the hand in the glove that does it. Yes, that is so. I tell you that we are nothing but gloves. The hand in the glove is the Holy Spirit of God. Can the glove do something if it is very near the hand? No! The glove must be filled with the hand to do the work. That is exactly the same for us: We must be filled with the Holy Spirit to do the work God has for us to do."[1]

Examining the Heart

While it is the Holy Spirit that gives us the power to change the words we speak, the desire to change begins in the heart. The Bible says:

> Make a tree good and its fruit will be good, or make a tree bad and its fruit will be bad, for a tree is recognized by its fruit…For out of the overflow of the heart the mouth speaks. The good man brings good things out of the good stored up in him, and the evil man brings evil out of the evil stored up in him. But I tell you that men will have to give account on the day of judgment for every careless word they have spoken. For by your words you will be acquitted and by your words you will condemned (Matthew 12:33-37).

The word "heart" that is used in this passage is from the Greek word *kardia*. It is not referring to the blood-pumping muscle in the chest cavity, but to our thoughts, motives, feelings; our will; and our character. The *kardia* is the seat of our emotions and represents the inner person. The words that escape our lips reveal the condition of inner man.

Remember the children's song:

> *I'm a little teapot short and stout,*
> *Here is my handle, here is my spout.*
> *When I get all steamed up, hear me shout,*
> *Just tip me over and pour me out.*

Well, I don't know about you, but when I get all steamed up, what comes out of my mouth isn't always a cup of tea! It's in those unguarded moments of frustration, anger, or pain that our mouths tend to spew out what is really inside. Jesus said, "What goes into a man's mouth does not make him 'unclean,' but what comes out of his mouth, that is what makes him 'unclean'...The things that come out of the mouth come from the heart, and these make a man 'unclean'" (Matthew 15:11,18). Jesus continually pointed out the condition of the Pharisees' hearts. They clung to outward religious practices, but what God desired most, their hearts, were hardened and cold.

Every thought is a seed. If you plant crabapples, don't count on harvesting Golden Delicious.

—AUTHOR UNKNOWN

In the book of Isaiah, the prophet used the example of the people's speech to point to their condition: "Everyone is ungodly and wicked, every mouth speaks vileness" (Isaiah 9:17). The lips are the crack from which the condition of the heart seeps.

We cannot act beyond what we believe. Therefore, if we want to change the way we speak, I believe the first step is to check on the condition of the heart. In the Old Testament, God spoke about the transforming power that would be available to His people through Jesus Christ. "I will give them an undivided heart and put a new spirit in them; I will remove from them their heart of stone and give them a heart of flesh. Then they will follow my decrees and be careful to keep my laws. They will be my people, and I will be their God" (Ezekiel 11:19-20).

This new covenant and new spirit was poured out at Pentecost and continues to flow today. "Through his death for sin once for all, Christ, the Mediator of the new covenant (Hebrews 8:6), has made it possible for all believers to receive the Spirit's divine enablement so that they too may believe according to God's righteous standards. This is available to all who place their faith in the resurrected Messiah, Jesus Christ."[2]

The book of Proverbs has much to say about how the condition of our hearts affects our speech:

- Above all else, guard your *heart,* for it is the wellspring of life (Proverbs 4:23).

- The wise in *heart* accept commands, but a *chattering* fool comes to ruin (Proverbs 10:8).

- A prudent man keeps his knowledge to himself, but the *heart* of fools blurts out folly (Proverbs 12:23).

- An anxious *heart* weights a man down, but a kind *word* cheers him up (Proverbs 12:25).

- The discerning *heart* seeks knowledge, but the *mouth* of a fool feeds on folly (Proverbs 15:14).

- The *heart* of the righteous weighs its answers, but the *mouth* of the wicked gushes evil (Proverbs 15:28 TNIV).

- A cheerful look brings joy to the *heart,* and *good news* gives health to the bones (Proverbs 15:30).

- The wise in *heart* are called discerning, and *pleasant words* promote instruction (Proverbs 16:21).

- The *hearts* of the wise make their *mouths* prudent, and their *lips* promote instruction (Proverbs 16:23 TNIV).

- One who loves a pure *heart* and who *speaks* with grace will have the king for a friend (Proverbs 22:11 TNIV).

- Like a coating of glaze over earthenware are fervent *lips* with an evil *heart* (Proverbs 26:23).

- Enemies disguise themselves with their *lips,* but in their *hearts* they harbor deceit. Though their speech is charming, do not believe them, for seven abominations fill their hearts (Proverbs 26:24-25 TNIV).

So, how's your heart? The heart of the matter is a matter of the heart.

Renewing the Mind

Have you ever been to a rodeo and watched a lassoing contest? The little calf bursts from the stall, and then the cowboy and his steed follow close behind. With his lasso in hand, the cowboy swings the rope in the air and attempts to catch the little heifer before she escapes out the corral door at the opposite side of the arena. That is a vivid picture of what we must do with the words that attempt to escape the gate (the mouth). We must rein them in.

The Bible teaches us to take captive every thought and make it obedient to Christ (2 Corinthians 10:3-5). Once we lasso a thought (take it captive), we can decide which words leave the gate and which words need to be tied up and secured. Studies show that we speak at about 120 to 180 words a minute.[3] Seems like we need to do a bit more lassoing and a lot less running on.

Let's take a look at this little heifer of words and how to rein it in. First, a thought bursts forth from the stall called the brain. It runs across the mind headed for the door called the mouth. In a split second we must determine if that thought is of God or if it is against the knowledge of God. If we determine that the words are not of

> *The mind of man is the battle-ground on which every moral and spiritual battle is fought.*
>
> —J. Oswald Sanders

God, then we lasso the thought and it never makes its way out of the gate. If it passes the God test, we allow it to go free.

What is the lasso? It is the Word of God—the Word of Truth. That can seem a bit overwhelming, so let's just pick two verses as our lasso. Philippians 4:8-9 is a great place to start.

Whatever is true, whatever is noble, whatever is right, whatever is pure, whatever is lovely, whatever is admirable—if anything is excellent or praiseworthy—think about such things. Whatever you have learned or received or heard from me, or seen in me—put it into practice. And the God of peace will be with you.

Before we speak, we should ask ourselves:

- Are they true? Are these words reliable, certain, in accordance with fact, exact, and accurate? Do they line up with God's truth? For example, when we speak negatively about someone, we should consider: Do these words fit with God's view of this person as His image bearer?

- Are they noble? Because I am a child of the King, my words should reflect nobility. Is what I am about to say demonstrating high moral character or ideals? Is it language that exhibits excellent qualities or a person with royal rank?

- Are they right? Are these words virtuous, in accordance with fact and not assumption? Are they appropriate, suitable, and reputable? Right words at the wrong time become wrong words. Is this the right time, or do I need to wait for a more appropriate time?

- Are they pure? Are these words free from anything that taints, or infects the reputation of another? Are these words tainted by my own sin, or do they reflect the righteousness of Christ that has been given to me?

- Are they lovely? Do these words inspire love, affection, or admiration? Are they morally or spiritually attractive or gracious? Do these words conjure up a picture of beauty or loveliness?

- Are they admirable? Do these words inspire others to see excellent qualities in another person? Do the words paint a picture of praise or excellence?

- Are they excellent? Do these words reflect goodness, exceptional merit, or virtue? Are they of a high moral nature? Would God rank them as "excellent" if they were spoken?

- Are they praiseworthy? Do these words stir a sense of praise or condemnation?

Now that is a lot to think about, considering that the mind thinks about 130 words per minute. It is unlikely that we will have the time or the wherewithal to filter every word that proceeds from our minds to our mouths through this eight-layer sieve. However, Paul doesn't just leave us with the qualifying list; he gives us the means by which to implement it. "Whatever you have learned or received or heard from me, or seen in me—*put it into practice.*"

It takes practice! Practice! Practice! Practice!

But look at the result: "And the God of peace will be with you."

The King James Version of 2 Corinthians 10:5 says it this way: "*Casting down* imaginations, and every high thing that exalteth itself against the knowledge of God, and bringing into captivity every thought to the obedience of Christ." I like that picture of casting down. Once the cowboy slips the lasso around the calf's neck, he throws her to the ground and whips that rope around her kicking legs to make sure she's not going anywhere. Likewise, we need to cast down those thoughts back to the dirt where they came from and make sure *they* aren't going anywhere.

Lord, make my words gracious and tender, for tomorrow I may have to eat them!

—AUTHOR UNKNOWN

While we've got the picture of cowboys and cattle in our minds, let's look at another animal in the corral—the horse. Paul compares the tongue to a bridle in a horse's mouth. "When we put bits into the mouths of horses to make them obey us we can turn the whole animal...Likewise the tongue is a small part of the body, but it makes great boasts" (James 3:3,5). Our words, like a bit in a horse's mouth, can control the course we travel. They can pull us to the left or the right...all depending on who is holding the reins to which the bit is attached. But sometimes, it seems that horse just gets away from us and needs to be reined back in.

Taming the Tongue

Martha is a sweet older woman who is in the intermediate stages of Alzheimer's disease. Perhaps one of the most radical changes in her behavior, besides memory loss, is her inability to control her tongue. Martha has always used her words in a positive way, but in these latter years her words have become unrestrained. Her ability to keep unkind or hurtful words from escaping her lips is impaired. She can't help it. It's part of the disease that is ravaging her mind. But watching my dear friend has helped me realize the importance of restraining our tongues. It is a sign of physical, spiritual, and emotional health.

When I was young, I loved reading the story of a stately steed named Black Beauty. In my early teens, I enjoyed visiting my friend Cammie and riding horses on her parents' dairy farm. We often clicked our heels and raced through the fields with reckless abandonment.

The horse is a powerful animal, yet with the tug of the reins or the tap of a heel, he will submit to his master's bidding. On the other hand, a wild stallion that has not been brought under control of a master is of very little use.

In the Bible we are instructed to have a spirit of gentleness, which tempers the words we speak (Galatians 5:23). The Greek word for "gentleness" is *prautes* and suggests a wild horse that has been tamed. Unfortunately, in our modern society the word "gentleness" connotes being weak. However, the Greek word means anything but weak. Picture a muscular steed, proudly holding his head, poised to move with speed and power, nostrils flaring, but at the same time under his master's control. That is a true picture of *prautes*—gentleness.

The same word, *prautes,* is translated "meek" in the King James Version. When Jesus said He was "meek and lowly in heart" (Matthew 11:29), He was saying He was submitted to God—mightily powerful but under God's control. Only when we submit our tongues to God will we have the ability to use our words for good. Meekness isn't weakness; it's power under control. It's taming and training our tongues to be under the submission and control of the Holy Spirit.

Let me give you an example. Oh, I hate to admit this, but I fear many sisters will relate—the dents in my armor attest to it.

Before I became a Christian, I was "gifted" with a quick sarcastic wit. Have you ever been in an argument and two hours later thought of a great comeback or slam remark? Not me. I could think of them on the spot. I was good—so good. Why, I could have opened up a side business feeding disgruntled wives, employees, and friends quick comebacks through earphones during confrontations. However, after I accepted Christ as my Savior, it didn't take the Holy Spirit long to convict me that my tongue was not glorifying God.

Sure, it brought some laughs, but Jesus wasn't smiling. So I began the arduous task of taming my tongue. It was hard letting all those good sarcastic comments go to waste, but I knew they were only fit for the garbage heap.

That was more than 30 years ago. On many occasions, when someone is telling me about a confrontation with a family member or a coworker, those quick-witted remarks still pop up in my mind like a cue card on a stage. When a store clerk offers a snide remark, I can usually think of one snider. So where's the victory? The victory comes when I choose not to let the words out of my mouth. When I lasso the words before they have a chance to run out of the gate. When I offer blessings rather than cursing. When I put on the humility of Christ and take the comments without the retaliation. That, my friend, is choosing to walk in the Spirit instead of choosing to walk in the flesh. It can only happen by the power of the Holy Spirit and becomes easier with practice.

Retraining Our Reflexes

It was hot. The traffic was heavy. I was young and distracted.

I was driving alone in the flow of traffic traveling to and from the North Carolina coast. I was in the group headed for home. The July traffic was bumper-to-bumper with everyone going faster than the posted speed limit. I had other things on my mind besides maneuvering in traffic and was paying little attention to the cars around me.

Traveling 60 mph in my sporty two-toned Pontiac Sunbird, I felt my front right tire slip off the asphalt and onto the gravel shoulder of the road. In a flood of panic, I heard the voice of my driver's ed teacher from four years before, "If you run off the road, do not, and I repeat, do not jerk your car back on the road. Slow down to a stop and then gently guide the car back onto the road."

My mind knew the rule. I was even repeating, "Do not jerk the car, do not jerk the car." Then I promptly jerked the car. I pulled the steering wheel to the left, jerked the car onto the road, and lost control. First the Sunbird flew across two lanes of traffic to the left and then, after overcorrecting again, she flew back off the road to the right. As if in slow motion, the car began a descent down an embankment. The weight of the car became unbalanced and began to roll. As the car somersaulted down the embankment, my body tossed and tumbled like a rag doll, bouncing around the car's interior. I wasn't wearing my seat belt. When the car landed upside down at the bottom of the embankment, I was sitting on the ceiling of the passenger's side.

Travelers watched with mouths aghast as the scenario played out before them. You can imagine how amazed they were to see me crawl out of the car's opened window without a scratch. I knew, without a doubt, that I should not have lived through that accident. It was only by the grace of God that I survived.

Thinking back on that event, I am reminded how powerful reflexes are. When the car veered off the road, I knew what to do, but I did the opposite. I knew not to jerk the steering wheel, but I did it regardless.

When it comes to changing the way we speak, we may have some very powerful reflexes to overcome. The Bible tells us that when we come to Christ, we are a new creation (2 Corinthians 5:17). However, no one pushes the delete button to erase the old habit patterns that have been formed over time. That comes with practice, training, and reprogramming.

I want to encourage you not to become discouraged if you make a mistake and use your words in a negative way from time to time. Satan would like nothing better than for you to simply give up on using your words for good. But even Jesus knew that sometimes a temple has to be cleaned out more then once.

Shortly after Jesus' first miracle at the wedding of Cana, He traveled to Capernaum with His mother, brothers, and disciples. It was almost time for the Jewish Passover celebration, so Jesus went up to Jerusalem to worship. As He approached the temple, Jesus heard the bleating of sheep, smelled the stench of the cattle, and saw the gypsylike haggling and exchanging of coins. The temple had become a free-for-all rather than a house of prayer.

"So he made a whip out of cords, and drove all from the temple area, both sheep and cattle; he scattered the coins of the money changers and overturned their tables. To those who sold doves he said, 'Get these out of here! How dare you turn my Father's house into a market!'" (John 2:15-16).

Yes, Jesus cleaned out the temple that day, but it wasn't long before the money changers began to creep back in with their wares. I imagine it all began with one man setting up his table. Then another and another until the carnival-type atmosphere once again polluted God's house.

This incident recorded in John 2 occurred at the beginning of Jesus' earthly ministry. But we see a similar scene toward the end. It was just a few days before Jesus' arrest and crucifixion. He rode into town on a donkey as the crowd spread their cloaks on the road. "Blessed is the king who comes in the name of the Lord!" they shouted as Jesus passed by.

Once Jesus arrived in Jerusalem, He headed straight for the temple area to worship. Once again He was met with mayhem and stench of the money changers and the animals they sold for temple sacrifices. As He had done three years earlier, Jesus began driving out the money changers with their doves, sheep, and cattle scampering behind. "It is written, 'My house will be a house of prayer,' but you have made it a den of robbers!"

In the New Testament, God calls us temples of the living God (2 Corinthians 6:16). Just as Jesus cleaned the temple at the beginning and the end of His earthly ministry, so we may need to clean out our temples many times. Yes, we make a clean sweep of the sin in our lives on the day we accept Jesus as our Savior, but those bad habits will try to creep back in if the temple is left unattended. So check up on yourself often. Pay attention to your words and determine if you need a spring-cleaning to keep the temple pure.

Psychologists tell us that it takes 21 days to establish a new habit.

Here's an idea. For 21 days put five pennies in your left pocket. Each time you say an encouraging word to someone, move a penny to the right pocket. Make it your goal to move all the pennies from the left to the right and deposit encouraging words to those you come in contact with each day. You'll be doing more than moving pennies. You'll be investing in another's soul.

James wrote, "If anyone considers himself religious and yet does not keep a tight rein on his tongue, he deceives himself and his religion is worthless" (James 1:26). Although James uses the analogy of a horse when teaching on the tongue, he's not horsing around when it comes to the impact the tongue has on those around us. I'm just chomping at the bit to get started with specifics of changing the direction this filly is headed, so let's rein in our words and gallop on down the path to changing the way we speak—and get specific.

*T*HE *P*RODUCT OF *P*RACTICE

Think all you speak, but speak not all you think.

—PATRICK DELANEY

ONE OF MY FAVORITE PLACES to spend time with God each morning is on my patio overlooking the morning sun dancing from the pristine lake off my backyard. On one particular morning I was enjoying a fresh cup of coffee and God's Word. My flower gardens were at their peak, bursting with fuchsia, red, and white impatiens, begonias, and blue ageratum. The hanging baskets next to my patio chair were heavy with purple and pink velvet petunias, filling the air with a sweet fragrance not found in the finest department stores. It was one of those perfect peaceful storybook mornings.

I sat down close enough to the baskets to keep the scent of the petunias wafting past my nose. Suddenly, a little finch darted from the flower basket which had become his summer residence. He perched on a tree in front of me, furious that I had invaded his space, and angrily began rapid-fire squawking in my direction. His bride came and perched beside him and sang a lovely song, but there was no chance of calming her man. He hopped around from the tree, to the chair, to the wall, to the table. Pointing his beak in my direction and with ruffled feathers he squawked at me.

Get out of here! he seemed to say. *You are invading my space!* My effort to ignore this little bird did not squelch his effort to drive me away.

Finally, after 45 minutes of this constant badgering, I could take it no longer and decided to give this bird a piece of my mind. "Look, buddy, who planted those flower baskets in the first place? I did! Who hung and fertilized them? I did! And who waters them daily? I do! Don't you come out here complaining to me because I chose to sit here and enjoy what I've planted. They're mine in the first place—not yours. I'm just letting you live there. And you should be thankful for that! Besides, you're making a terrible mess!"

The more I reminded him of why he should be thankful and stop his complaining, the more he squawked.

I attempted to have my time alone with the Lord anyway. What verse should I read but Psalm 24:1 (NASB): "The earth is the LORD's and all it contains. The world, and those who dwell in it. For He has founded it upon the seas and established it upon the rivers."

Suddenly those angry squawks from the finch had a familiar ring to them. They sounded—as a matter of fact—a lot like my own voice!

Oh, how I complain when someone messes up my plans, when situations don't go my way, when someone invades my space. My space. My plans. My way. My, my, my.

Then I heard another voice speaking to my heart from my heavenly Father. *Who made this earth in the first place? Who planted and watered all you have before you? I knew the days for you before you were even born (Psalm 139:16). I've mapped them out. This whole earth is Mine and all that it contains. I'm just letting you live here. And sometimes you make a terrible mess. Stop your squawking and start chirping the song that I've put in your heart.*

God had sent His messenger in the form of a feathered finch to remind me just how annoying my complaining and squawking can be. Oh, dear sister, let's stop using our words to screech, scream, and squall. Instead, let's chirp, cheer, and cry out with words that glorify God and make others glad that we've perched on their day for a while.

Examining the Words We Speak

Ephesians 4:29 (NASB) is a wonderful plumb line for the words we speak. "Let no unwholesome word proceed from your mouth, but only such a word as is good for edification according to the need of the moment, so that it will give grace to those who hear." Another version says, "Let no foul or polluting language, nor evil word or unwholesome or worthless talk [ever] come out of your mouth, but only such [speech] as is good and beneficial to the spiritual progress of others, as is fitting to the need and the occasion, that it may be a blessing and give grace (God's favor) to those who hear it" (AMP). If that were the guiding principle for each one of us, the world would certainly be a quieter place!

We've looked at where the power to change comes from. Now let's examine specific ways we can tame the tongue.

Anger to Aroma

Anger—we all know what it looks and sounds like. The kids track mud through the house again, a husband forgets an anniversary, a car pulls out in front of us and putters down the road at 20 mph, the oven decides to stop working one hour before dinner guests are scheduled to arrive. How do we react? With anger!

The Greek word for "anger" is *orge* and means "any natural impulse, or desire, or disposition," and came to be known as anger— the strongest of all passions.[1] While the culture says that anger is healthy, the Bible tells us to rid ourselves of it (Colossians 3:8).

I was with a friend who was being treated very unfairly. Someone had approached her about coauthoring a book. Plans were made, contracts were discussed, and content was already forming in her mind. But then she received a phone call from the spouse of the coauthor, who stopped the project.

Several people were in earshot of this conversation. I was upset that my friend was being treated in such a manner! However, rather than react in anger or defend herself, my friend graciously and with the love of Christ spoke words of kindness. Rather than becoming angry, she exuded the fragrance of Christ and it permeated the entire office.

That is the choice we have. When we choose not to react in anger, but extend grace, the aroma of Christ is released. "My dear brothers and sisters," Paul writes, "take note of this: Everyone should be quick to listen, slow to speak and *slow to become angry,* because our anger does not produce the righteousness that God desires" (James 1:19 TNIV). Thomas Jefferson once said, "If angry, count to ten before you speak; if very angry, one hundred."

Evil tongues are the devil's bellows.

—JOHN TRAPP

Where does anger come from, anyway? It is a reaction to irritating people and circumstances, you might say. But I believe that the root cause of anger is self-centeredness. We live in a world that tells us "It's all about me!" And when something doesn't suit the center of our universe—me—then anger erupts. That's difficult to admit, isn't it? Here's a little test. Each time you become angry over the next few days, ask yourself this question: Am I angry because I didn't get what I wanted when I wanted it?

Wow! When we ask that question, the little kid throwing a temper tantrum in the toy store bears a striking resemblance to the woman in the mirror we look at each day!

Rather than using our words in anger, we can use our words to be the fragrance of Christ (2 Corinthians 2:15). Have you ever hugged someone and ended up wearing her perfume? We will leave a fragrance, so to speak, by the words we speak.

Bitter to Better

"She's just a bitter old woman!" Have you ever heard someone described in that way? I have. And, amazingly, when someone uses the word "bitter," I know exactly what they mean. My dictionary defines bitter as "galling; exhibiting intense animosity, harshly reproachful, marked by cynicism and rancor." Bitterness stems from deep-seated anger and unforgiveness that plants itself into a soul and is watered and fertilized by playing and replaying the video of the offense in the theater of the mind.

Paul warns us that having a "bitter root" can grow up and "defile many" (Hebrews 12:15). James tell us that bitterness is from the devil (James 3:14-15). And Peter cautions that bitterness can keep us from being effective in ministry (Acts 8:20-23).

Bitterness in our hearts will produce bitterness in our actions. (Consider Naomi in the story of Ruth.) The only way to be free of bitterness is to let go of past offenses and refuse to collect them. Collect antiques, Beanie Babies, or even shoes. But don't collect grudges. There's not enough storage space in your heart to bear the load. Grudges will tumble out every time the door to your mouth is opened.

"My mother used to be a bitter woman," Tom explained. "But then she got Alzheimer's disease and forgot what she was so bitter about. She actually became a very pleasant person to be around."

Rather than growing bitter, choose to be better!

The fact is, hurt is inevitable in relationships. We are sinful creatures living in a fallen world, and only by the grace of God can we be a blessing to anyone. The only way to be better rather than bitter is to extend the same grace to others that God extended to us through Jesus Christ. The key to writing a beautiful life story is to have a pencil with a good eraser.

If ever there was a person who had the right to be bitter, it was Joseph in the Bible. He was thrown in a pit and left for dead, sold into slavery by his jealous brothers, falsely accused of attempted rape, forgotten by his friends, and unjustly detained in a prison cell for many years. After his release and subsequent appointment as governor of Egypt, he came face-to-face with the very brothers who caused his demise. Rather than give them the punishment they deserved, he said, "You intended to harm me, but God intended it for good to accomplish what is now being done, the saving of many lives" (Genesis 50:20). Joseph chose not to be bitter, but to allow his circumstances to make him better. And with God's help, we can do the same.

> *He is richest who is content with the least.*
>
> —CHARLES SPURGEON

Complaining to Contentment

When I was 20 years old, I flew with five others to Nevis, West Indies, for a dental mission trip. Like six sardines packed into an aluminum can, we sat shoulder to shoulder in the rickety twin engine plane. The mission was to provide dental care for the poverty-stricken natives of a tiny island with 90 percent unemployment.

With a newly acquired degree in dental hygiene, I was thrilled to join a dentist and his team for a week of ministering to the men, women, and children of this tropical island. We had so much to give to a people who had so little...or so I thought.

The plane that took us over to the island was so tiny that we could not take our equipment and our luggage in the same trip. We all decided (or the men did) that we didn't really need our clothes. They loaded the equipment and our clothes were to follow later in the day. Our motto became, "Tell me what you need, and I'll tell you how you can do without it."

Even without our luggage, the plane was slightly overloaded. I, being the lightest of the bunch, was relegated to the copilot's seat. I just kept telling myself that if we crashed, I'd be the first to see Jesus, so that was okay with me.

What did we encounter on the island? There was poverty. There were many dental needs. I expected that. What I did not expect was the sense of contentment and joy I saw on the faces of the 12 children who lived in a one-room thatched shack with no running water and a packed dirt floor, the contentment of the woman who had one dress to wear, the satisfaction of the men who filled their bellies with food from the ocean and tropical fruit that sprang from the surrounding flora. I did not expect the incredible praises to God that rose through the church roofs, the laughter of children dressed in tattered rags, or the coos of mothers contentedly holding their babies to their breasts. I had arrogantly come to help these people, but they had helped me. I experienced what Charles Surgeon penned: "He is richest who is content with the least."

From my earliest years of adulthood, God allowed me to see contentment through the lives of the poor. I knew contentment would never be attained through achievement, accumulation of wealth, or accolades from others. And yet all through my life there has been the tension of complaining and contentment.

The man who forgets to be thankful has fallen asleep in life.

—ROBERT LOUIS STEVENSON.

Why? I believe it all started in the Garden of Eden and continues today. Eve had it all but wasn't content. She believed God was holding out on her and ate the forbidden fruit.

Job was a man who lost everything, yet he did not complain. His wife, on the other hand, suggested he curse God and die (Job 2:9). But Job's reply was, "You are talking like a foolish woman. Shall we accept good from God and not trouble?" His contentment did not rely on people, position, or possessions, but on the knowledge of the sovereignty of God.

In the New Testament we see a mirrored example in the person of Paul. Paul had been a man of influence who graduated from the best schools with a degree of a Pharisee and had been born into the elite line of Benjamin. He referred to himself as a faultless Hebrew of Hebrews with legalistic righteousness. But after he came to Christ, not before, his life was riddled with persecution, problems, and prison. Yet he wrote, "I have learned to be content whatever the circumstances. I know what it is to be in need, and I know what it is to have plenty. I have learned the secret of being content in any and every situation, whether well fed or hungry, whether living in plenty or in want. I can do everything through him who gives me strength" (Philippians 4:11-13). Where was Paul when he penned these words? He was under house arrest, chained to a Roman soldier 24 hours a day. Paul knew that living in union with Christ was the true source of contentment. Amazingly, in this letter to the Philippians his key message is "Rejoice!"

Imagine yourself in prison for sharing the gospel. Would your tendency be to say, "God, this isn't fair. Why are You allowing this?" I'm ashamed to say that would be mine.

Come to think about it, I don't have to imagine it. I remember one weekend when I was flying to Houston for a speaking engagement. An hour into the trip, a woman on the plane passed out. The two doctors on board revived the embarrassed passenger and surmised that her blood sugar was probably low because she had not eaten breakfast. But protocol demanded that the plane had to land and disembark the damsel in distress. The closest airport was back from whence we came. My heart sank as I watched the clouds and realized the plane was turning around.

Two hours later, the same plane full of the same passengers minus one took off again. All of us with connecting flights in Dallas missed our connections and were rebooked on a later flight. The only problem was the flight, which was the last one out for the evening, had 32 passengers on standby. There was no way we were going to make the flight, and I was going to miss the speaking engagement that had been booked and prayed over for one year.

"God," I whined, "I am doing this for You! Why are You doing this? Why did You allow this to happen?"

In tears I called my husband to explain the situation. "I don't want to be doing this. It's not worth it. I want to be home with you. I am hungry, I am tired, and I am mad." On and on I went as Steve listened to my complaining.

Sitting at the gate with the crowd of disgruntled travelers who were also not going to make the flight, one man stood up and said, "I'm going to go rent a car and drive to Houston." Then a woman jumped up and added, "Can I go with you?" "Me too," a young businessman chimed in.

I joined this band of weary travelers and headed to the car rental booth. In the end, six strangers piled into a van with one common goal...get to Houston. During the two-hour trip, we addressed the usual questions about family and jobs and interests. The woman who sat beside me was a cheerleading coach. I felt she was just a little bit too perky considering the circumstances. I learned that she was headed to a competition, her kids were her life, and her husband...well, he was somewhere down the priority list between grocery shopping and housecleaning. But for two hours we chatted. She asked about my books, and when I mentioned one title, *Becoming the Woman of His Dreams,* she faltered.

"My husband would like for me to read that one," she mumbled.

"Oh, really? Why?" I inquired.

I cracked the door and she flung it wide open. Why not? I was a stranger and she would most likely never see me again. But for now, I was "chained to a Roman guard" as she confided in me what was going on in her marriage.

When we reached Houston, the driver didn't pull up to the airport and let us out. No, he drove me to the front door of the hotel, just in time for me to walk up to the podium for the women's conference. As I crawled out of the car and waved goodbye, I realized that the assignment from God wasn't about to commence when I walked into that hotel. It had begun the moment I walked out my front door. The delays were no accident. They were part of God's plan for my weekend assignment.

When we look at the difficulties, inconveniences, and problems of life as potential assignments from God, our perspective changes. We can decide to focus on what God can do through a difficult circumstance rather than the details of the circumstance itself.

During Paul's time chained to a Roman guard, he was not only captive, but he had a captive audience. He was able to have one-on-one time with some of the most influential Roman citizens...the guards. Not only was he able to share the gospel with them, but they were privy to the conversations between Paul and his many visitors from the churches. Paul's time in prison also gave him time to write letters to the churches, which we hold in our hands today in the New Testament.

> *What is in the well of your heart will show up in the bucket of your speech.*
>
> —AUTHOR UNKNOWN

Paul's words, "I can do all things through Him who strengthens me" (Philippians 4:13 NASB), was one of the first Bible verses I learned as a new Christian. I applied it to every hurdle imaginable. But the truth is, Paul wrote this verse in the context of contentment. How do we discover the secret to the contented life? How do we frame the words that come out of our mouths and influence those around us? "I can do all things through Him who strengthens me."

Can we be content if we never marry? Can we be content if our children don't turn out the way we had hoped? Can we be content if our bosses fail to see our potential? Can we be content if our parents continue to have unrealistic expectations for their adult children?

Let's take it down a notch...Can we be content if the waiter doesn't give good service? Can we be content if the line at the post office moves too slowly? Can we be content if our neighbor's dog keeps us up at night?

Words of contentment have great power because they make people sit up and take notice. They wonder...*what makes her different?* What are your words telling the world?

Fear to Faith

We all have times when our faith begins to waver and doubts creep in like slow-growing moss. Even Jesus' cousin John the Baptist had a bout with doubt. Remember John? He was born several months before Jesus for the sole purpose of preparing the way for Jesus' ministry. "Repent, for the kingdom of heaven is near" (Matthew 3:2). When Jesus approached John preaching and baptizing by the river, John announced, "Look, the Lamb of God, who takes away the sin of the world!" (John 1:29). John heard the voice of God saying, "This is my Son, whom I love; with him I am well pleased" (Matthew 3:17).

And yet, when John was arrested and sat alone in a dark prison cell, doubts began to creep in. He sent two of his friends to ask Jesus, "Are you the one who was to come, or should we expect someone else?" (Luke 7:18).

Jesus did not rebuke John for his bout with doubt, but rather reassured him to have faith and cling to the truth.

Faith is trusting God's heart when we can't trace His hand.

For close to a year I've been working in a large needlepoint piece that will hopefully one day be transformed into a piano bench cushion. The project keeps me company while traveling on airplanes or winding down in the quiet of a hotel room. The in and out rhythm of the needle relaxes my mind and helps the thoughts stop spinning around my little head.

I must say, the canvas is turning out quite lovely. But if you turn it over and look at the back side, it's a mess of tangles, knots, and frayed ends. That's the way it is with our lives at times. We tend to look at the underside of tangles, knots, and frayed ends, while G sees the finished product. Consider the words of this anony poem quoted by Corrie ten Boom in her book *Tramp for*

My life is but a weaving, between my God and me,
I do not choose the colors, He worketh steadily,
Oftimes He weaveth sorrow, and I in foolish pride,
Forget He sees the upper, and I the underside.
Until the loom is silent, and shuttles cease to fly,
Will God unfold the canvas and explain the reason why.
The dark threads are as needful in the skillful Weaver's hand,
As the threads of gold and silver in the pattern He has planned.[2]

If ever there was a woman who had a messy life, it was Rahab. Rahab was a prostitute who lived in one of the dwellings built into the walls of Jericho. When Joshua sent two spies into the city to scope out their enemies, the men went to Rahab's home. Jericho was a bustling city, and it was not uncommon for travelers to seek the house of a prostitute for lodging.

Rahab did not have the luxury of being taught the Scriptures as we do today. And yet she had faith in God because of what she had heard. When the king's men came looking for the Israelite spies, she hid them under stalks of flax on the roof. Rahab lived among people who were filled with fear because of the reputation of the Israelites and their God. But rather than being filled with fear, she made a proclamation of faith:

> I know that the Lord has given this land to you and that
> a great fear of you has fallen on us, so that all who live in
> this country are melting in fear because of you. We have
> heard how the Lord dried up the water of the Red Sea
> for you when you came out of Egypt, and what you did to
> Sihon and Og, the two kings of the Amorites east of the
> Jordan, whom you completely destroyed. When we heard of
> melted and everyone's courage failed because
> D your God is God in heaven above and
> . Now then, please swear to me by the
> ill show kindness to my family, because I
> less to you (Joshua 2:9-12).

Rahab turned her fear into faith. The power of her words saved her and her family, and they were assimilated into God's chosen people. Amazingly, Rahab became the mother of Boaz, the grandmother of Obed, the great-grandmother of Jesse, and finally the great-great-grandmother of King David. Her tiny branch is even part of Jesus' family tree.

I love this inscription posted at Hind's Head Inn in Bray, England: "Fear knocked at the door. Faith answered, and no one was there." Fear comes knocking with a thought. Faith answers with a word... God's Word. As Martin Luther wrote in his masterful "A Mighty Fortress Is Our God,": "One little word shall fell him." The very name of Jesus will defeat the devil and drive away fear.

Grumbling to Grateful

Grumbling is as old as Methuselah. Actually, it goes all the way back before him. After Satan enticed Eve to disobey God and eat the forbidden fruit, there was a whole lot of grumbling going on.

"The wife You gave me made me do it," Adam complained.

"The serpent You created made me do it," Eve whined.

And the grumbling didn't stop there. From Genesis to Revelation the grumbling rolls like a human freight train.

Perhaps one of the most vivid portraits of grumbling is found in Exodus when Moses led the Israelites out of Egypt. God's chosen people had been in servitude to the Egyptians for 400 years. During that time they had been "fruitful and multiplied greatly." They were "exceedingly numerous, so that the land was filled with them" (Exodus 1:7). Pharaoh feared that the Israelites would rebel and attempt to take over the kingdom, so he made them slaves in order to thwart a future uprising.

For 400 years the Israelites served under the whip of Egyptian taskmasters. Then one day God took note of their affliction and heard their cries for deliverance. So God chose Moses to be the deliverer of the Hebrew nation. What follows Moses' encounter with God at the burning bush in Midian is one of the most powerful stories in Scripture. Moses did indeed lead more than a million Israelites out of Egypt and on toward the Promised Land of Canaan.

But there were many roadblocks along the way, including the Hebrews' grumbling and unbelief. They grumbled because the drinking water was bitter, so God made it sweet (Exodus 15:23-25). They grumbled about the lack of food, so God brought forth manna from heaven (Exodus 16). They grumbled about the lack of meat, so God rained down quail from the sky (Exodus 16). Again, they grumbled because of the lack of water, so God caused water to spring from a rock (Exodus 17). They grumbled about the leadership selection, so God caused Aaron's rod, a dead piece of wood, to bud, bloom, and bear fruit (Numbers 17:8).

How did God feel about their grumbling and complaining?

> Now the people complained about their hardships in the hearing of the LORD, and when he heard them his anger was aroused. Then fire from the LORD burned among them and consumed some of the outskirts of the camp. When the people cried out to Moses, he prayed to the LORD and the fire died down (Numbers 11:1-2).

You would have thought they would learn their lesson from this singeing experience. But, unfortunately, while God's wrath burned the camp, it did not brand the message on their hearts. Finally, God had had enough of their grumbling, and even Moses' prayers could not stop His wrath. He forbade that generation to enter the Promised Land, and they died in the desert of unbelief and grumbling (Number 14:26-35). However, the next generation learned from their parents' mistakes. They worshipped the Lord, praised Him for His provisions, and believed His promises.

Here's what the first generation of freed Israelites did not understand. When they grumbled and complained, they were not speaking against Moses. They were speaking against God. "You are not grumbling against us," Moses said, "but against the LORD" (Exodus 16:8). God had miraculously delivered them from slavery, parted the Red

Sea, provided food from heaven, prevented their clothes and shoes from wearing out the entire time they were in the desert…and yet they grumbled.

Can you imagine such ingratitude? Unfortunately, I can. God provided a sacrifice for our sins and pardon from eternal damnation. "For God so loved the world that he gave his one and only Son, that whoever believes in him shall not perish but have eternal life" (John 3:16). And if that wasn't enough, there's more:

- God…*has given* us the Spirit as a deposit, guaranteeing what is to come (2 Corinthians 5:5).

- To each one of us grace *has been given* as Christ apportioned it (Ephesians 4:7).

- In his great mercy he *has given* us new birth into a living hope through the resurrection of Jesus Christ from the dead, and into an inheritance that can never perish, spoil or fade (1 Peter 1:3-4).

- His divine power *has given* us everything we need for life and godliness through our knowledge of him who called us by his own glory and goodness (2 Peter 1:3).

- He *has given* us his very great and precious promises, so that through them you may participate in the divine nature and escape the corruption in the world caused by evil desires (2 Peter 1:4).

- We know that we live in him and he in us, because he *has given* us of his Spirit (1 John 4:13).

- We know also that the Son of God has come and *has given* us understanding, so that we may know him who is true (1 John 5:20).

And yet we grumble and complain.

Could it be that when we grumble, we too are complaining, not simply about our circumstances, but about the sovereign God and His provisions for our lives?

It all boils down to our attitude and perspective of who is in control.

Bible teacher Chuck Swindoll says this about attitude:

> The longer I live, the more I realize the impact of attitude on life. Attitude, to me, is more important than facts. It is more important than the past, than money, than circumstances, than failures, than success, than what other people think or say or do. It is more important than appearance, giftedness or skill. It will make or break a company...a church...a home, or an individual. The remarkable thing is we have a choice every day regarding the attitude we will embrace for the day. We cannot change our past...we cannot change the fact that people will act in a certain way. We cannot change the inevitable. The only thing we can do is play on the one string we have, and that is our attitude. I am convinced that life is ten percent what happens to me and ninety percent how I react to it. And so it is with you...we are in charge of our attitudes.

And what can we do to change grumbling into gratitude? "Give thanks is all circumstances" (1 Thessalonians 5:18). May we never be like the nine lepers who did not return to thank Jesus for restoring their rotting flesh to wholeness, but run with the one who was thankful and fell at Jesus' feet in grateful adoration.

These are just a few of the practical ways we can tame the tongue, but sometimes we simply need to keep it in the stall altogether. Let's keep going.

THE POTENCY OF SILENCE

A closed mouth gathers no foot.

—AUTHOR UNKNOWN

FROM THE TIME I COULD HOLD a crayon in my chubby little hand, I've enjoyed creating various "works of art." For my family and friends, my endeavors usually found their way under the Christmas tree and into their hands. One year it was macramé hanging plant holders. Another it was a menagerie of decoupage wooden boxes. Then there were the years of framed cross-stitch, ceramic nativity sets, and quilted pig and chicken pillows.

When I was 17, it was the year of the candle. Everyone from Grandma Edwards to my best friends at school received praying hand candles. For weeks I slaved over a hot stove, stirring melted wax, meticulously centering ten-inch wicks, then slowly pouring the red, green, or yellow molten material into inverted molds in the shape of praying hands. When the wax hardened, I burped the rubber mold and plopped out the candle. My kitchen looked like a prosthesis laboratory with hands littering the counters.

I was cooking up a fresh batch of hands when the doorbell rang. "Oh, my word!" I cried as I glanced at the clock on the oven. "Jim's here!"

I was having so much fun waxing and wicking that I forgot the time. I had a date at 7:30, and here I was in pink hot curlers and a paraffin-covered sweatshirt. I rushed through the kitchen, leaped over my dad, who had fallen asleep on the den floor in front of the television, and threw open the door.

"Hi, Jim," I huffed. "Come on in. I'm not ready."

"So I noticed," he said with a grin.

"I was cooking candles and lost track of time."

"You were what?"

"Never mind. Just come on in and have a seat on the couch. I'll be ready in a minute."

I dashed to my room to run a brush through my hair, swipe mascara through my lashes, and place a hint of gloss on my lips. Jim sat uncomfortably on the sofa, listening to my father snore to the bantering of Jackie Gleason and Ralph Kramden. After about 15 minutes, Jim smelled something burning. He didn't want to yell for me for fear of waking up my dad, so he tiptoed into the kitchen and discovered a pot sitting on the stove with flames shooting up about 18 inches in the air.

Sleeping dad or no sleeping dad, Jim called out. "Sharon! Whatever you were cooking is on fire!"

"Oh, my goodness!" I exclaimed. "I forgot to turn the stove off!"

Just as I burst into the kitchen, Jim threw a cup of water into the flaming wax. Rather then extinguish the flames, the fire exploded upward. The flames shot up the wall, across the ceiling, and down the wall on the other side of the room. Our screams woke my father to see his daughter standing in a room surrounded by flames. With the agility of Superman, Dad sprang to his feet, ran to the kitchen faster than a speeding bullet, grabbed the lid of the pot, and clamped it down on the source of the flames. Just as quickly as the fire had erupted, it receded back into the pot like a genie returning to his bottle.

This all happened in a matter of seconds. We stood in the middle of the room like three stunned deer. I never did tell my dad that it was Jim who threw the water on the burning wax. Teenage boys already have two strikes against them when they walk through the threshold to pick up a man's baby girl.

After the shock of the incident wore off, I had time to reflect on the incident: the speed at which the flames blazed around the room, the feeling of fire licking against my skin, the terrifying sound the fire made. I thought about my words and how easily they can explode and singe those around me. I saw and understood the destructive power of our words and the speed at which that destruction can spread. But you know what I also learned? I learned just how easy it is to stop the blaze…put a lid on it. As soon as my father placed a lid on the pot and removed the flames' source of oxygen, the fire abated. I think Job had the right idea when he said, "I will put my hand over my mouth" (Job 40:4). It is interesting to me that my hand fits perfectly over my mouth. Give it a try. How about you? Is your hand able to amply cover that spark-shooting orifice? Perhaps that was God's intentional design!

It took me back to James' comparison of the destructive power of our words: "Consider what a great forest is set on fire by a small spark" (James 3:5). In the last chapter we considered ways to transform the words we speak. But sometimes the most powerful words are the ones not spoken at all.

Silence Is Golden

Solomon wrote: "When words are many, sin is not absent, but he who holds his tongue is wise" (Proverbs 10:19). "Even a fool is thought wise if he keeps silent, and discerning if he holds his tongue" (Proverbs 17:28). Whether the subject is gossip or grumbling, silence is the golden key that keeps the door to destructive words locked away. And sometimes the most powerful words of a woman are no words at all, for silence can be an outward sign of inward strength.

I was having lunch with a group of friends when one made a derogatory comment about one of the group who was late. I gave her that "motherly look" that let her know the comment wasn't appropriate.

"Well, it's true," she said.

"Just because something is true doesn't mean that you should say it," I answered.

You know where I learned that? The Holy Spirit speaks that to me almost every day. Unfortunately, I have ignored Him more times than I'd like to admit, and I have spoken words I have later regretted. Like David, I plead with God to "set a guard over my mouth, O LORD; keep watch over the door of my lips" (Psalm 141:3).

> *God gave us teeth to hold back our tongue.*
> —OLD GREEK PROVERB

The summer before my senior year in high school, I went to France to study language and art with 50 or so students from around the United States. As part of our training, we were allowed to only speak French during mealtimes. If we slipped and said a word in English, we had to put a coin into a bowl in the middle of the table. It was the quietest bunch of teenagers sitting around a dinner table you've ever seen! In reality, saying an inappropriate word will cost more than a few coins. It can cost a relationship. Sometimes the most powerful words are no words at all.

A little girl lost a playmate in death, and one day reported to her family that she had gone to comfort the sorrowing mother. "What did you say?" asked her father. "Nothing," she replied. "I just climbed up on her lap and cried with her."

Gossip Is Deadly

A monster was sneaking into my yard in the dark of night and devouring my prize plants. I never saw his beady eyes or heard his pounding footsteps—just the aftermath of his destruction. He left a trail of slime as he moved from plant to plant, leaving large gaping holes in broad leaf gerbera daisies, gnawing entire velvety trumpet-shaped blossoms on purple petunias, and reducing bushy begonias to naked stalks.

I asked a neighbor about my flower bed's demise, and she said, "You've got slugs."

"Slugs!" I exclaimed. "The yard monster is a tiny little slug?"

"You can put out slug bait to catch them and see for yourself," my confident neighbor continued.

I sprinkled slug bait all around the yard and then waited. The next morning I viewed the "monsters'" remains. The beasts were about a quarter-inch long—about the size of my little toe nail.

How could something so small cause so much damage in such a short amount of time? I mused. Then my mind thought of something else very small that can cause enormous damage in a short amount of time...gossip. King Solomon wrote, "The words of a gossip are like choice morsels; they go down to a man's inmost parts" (Proverbs 18:8). Just as one tiny slug can destroy an entire flower bed, so can one tiny morsel of gossip destroy a person's reputation, mar one's character, and devour a friendship.

> *Blessed is the man (woman) who, having nothing to say, abstains from giving us wordy evidence of the fact.*
>
> —GEORGE ELIOT

In the South we have this knack for making gossips sound... almost nice. All you have to do is add "bless her heart" to the end of the sentence. It goes like this: "Susie gained fifty pounds with that last pregnancy, bless her heart." "Marcy's husband ran off with his secretary, bless her heart." "I heard Clair yelling at the postman yesterday, bless her heart." But all the "bless her hearts" don't mask what is really going on...gossip.

Solomon wrote, "Whoever repeats the matter separates close friends" (Proverbs 17:9 TNIV). Charles Allen, author of *God's Psychiatry*, observed: "Those of great minds discuss ideas, people of mediocre minds discuss events, and those of small minds discuss other people."[1] Maybe if we are spending our time talking about people, we need to fill our minds with better material, such as good books and other reading material (and I don't mean *People* magazine or the *Enquirer*).

What exactly is gossip? My dictionary defines gossip as "easy, fluent, trivial talk, talk about people behind their backs." It's repeating information about another person's private affairs. If you have to look around to make sure that no one can hear what you are saying, you are probably gossiping. If you would not say something in front of the person you are talking about, then you're probably gossiping.

We have often heard the phrase "knowledge is power." Perhaps that is why gossip is so appealing. It suggests a certain amount of power because "I have the inside scoop." But gossip is not power. On the contrary, it shows a lack of power...a lack of self-control.

But it takes two to tango the gossip dance. "Without wood the fire goes out; without gossip a quarrel dies down" (Proverbs 26:20). The Bible tells us to make every effort to avoid gossipers (Proverbs 20:19). A good rule of thumb is if you are not part of the problem or part of the solution, then keep the information to yourself.

Paul warned, "Some of you are living idle lives, refusing to work and wasting time meddling in other people's business" (2 Thessalonians 3:11 NLT). Other translations call such people "busybodies" (NASB, NIV).

One day a woman felt overwhelmed with guilt over her years of malicious gossip. She went to the local priest and confessed her sin. The priest was all too aware of her wagging tongue and had experienced the sting of her words firsthand...or rather secondhand.

"What can I do to rectify all the damage I have caused with my gossip?" she asked.

"Gather a bag of feathers," he began. "Then go around to each house and place a feather at their door."

That seemed like a simple enough request, so the woman did

just as the priest had instructed. After the task was complete, she returned. "I have done what you requested," she said. "Now what am I to do?"

"Now go back and retrieve each of the feathers," he replied.

"That is impossible," the woman argued. "The wind will have blown them all around town by now."

"Exactly," replied the wise priest. "Once you have spoken an ill word, it drifts through the air on wings of gossip, never to be retrieved. God has forgiven you, as you have asked. But I cannot remove the consequences of your hurtful words or gather them from the places they have landed."

Here's an idea. If a friend approaches you with some "news" or a "concern" about another person, stop and ask, "May I quote you on what you're about to tell me?" That will usually put a lid on the conversation before it even begins.

Wisdom Is Key

Solomon wrote, "To everything there is a season, and a time for every matter or purpose under heaven…a time to keep silent and a time to speak" (Ecclesiastes 3:1,7). Sometimes the most powerful words are the ones we do not speak. There is a time to speak and a time to keep quiet. The wise woman discerns the difference.

Proverbs 31 is one of my favorite chapters in the Bible. Verses 10-31 have served as a plumb line for women throughout the centuries. The verses were actually penned by King Lemuel's mother, instructing him about what to look for in a godly wife. The Proverbs 31 woman wasn't an actual person, but an ideal this wise mother set before her precious son. While the ideal can be quite intimidating to some, all would agree she is a role model worth emulating. Let's think for just a moment about the qualities of this treasured lady. Scripture describes her as smart, crafty, thrifty, and strong. She's a good cook, a savvy money manager, a helper in the community, an entrepreneur, a seamstress, a blessed mother, a faithful friend, a loyal wife, and a lover of God. Verse 10 begins, "An excellent wife, who can find? For her worth is far above jewels" (NASB). The NIV calls her "a wife of noble character." But I personally like the Amplified version, which says, "a capable, intelligent, and virtuous woman." The Hebrew word that's translated "excellent" or "virtuous" can also mean "wealthy, prosperous, valiant, boldly courageous, powerful, mighty warrior." That sounds strikingly like the *ezer* we met in chapter 5.

In order to help Lemuel remember these character traits, she taught them in the form of an acrostic using the Hebrew letters from A-Z. The queen knew that among the most important qualities to look for in a wife were the words she spoke. She instructed her son at her knee. "She speaks with wisdom and faithful instruction is on her tongue" (Proverbs 31:26).

Where does wisdom come from? Does it naturally come with gray hair as old wives' tales have said? Is it obtained through education? Is it a product of intelligence? King Solomon believed wisdom came from God. He sums it up this way, "The fear of the Lord is the beginning of wisdom, and knowledge of the Holy One is understanding" (Proverbs 9:10). Bottom line...wisdom comes from a reverence, knowledge, and understanding of God.

> *The deepest rivers flow with the least sound.*
>
> –QUINTUS CURTIUS RUFUS

But how does one define wisdom? The *New Open Bible* defines wisdom as "knowledge guided by understanding." It can also be defined as the "power of judging rightly and following the soundest course of action, based on knowledge, experience, understanding."

Consider the following verses about wisdom:

- The Lord gives wisdom, and from his mouth come knowledge and understanding (Proverbs 2:6).

- Wisdom will save you from the ways of wicked men, from men whose words are perverse (Proverbs 2:12).

- Blessed are those who find wisdom, those who gain understanding, for she is more profitable than silver and yields better returns than gold. She is more precious than rubies; nothing you desire can compare with her (Proverbs 3:13-15 TNIV).

- Do not forsake wisdom, and she will protect you; love her, and she will watch over you (Proverbs 4:6).

- Choose my instruction instead of silver, knowledge rather than choice gold, for wisdom is more precious than rubies, and nothing you desire can compare with her (Proverbs 8:10-11).

- The mouth of the righteous brings forth wisdom, but a perverse tongue will be cut out (Proverbs 10:31).

- When pride comes, then comes disgrace, but with humility comes wisdom (Proverbs 11:2).

- Pride only breeds quarrels, but wisdom is found in those who take advice (Proverbs 13:10).

- How much better to get wisdom than gold, to choose understanding rather than silver (Proverbs 16:16).

- A discerning person keeps wisdom in view, but a fool's eyes wander to the ends of the earth (Proverbs 17:24 TNIV).

So how do we obtain godly wisdom? It all begins with a personal relationship with Jesus Christ. Paul wrote, "In him [Jesus Christ], we have redemption through his blood, the forgiveness of sins, in accordance with the riches of God's grace that he lavished on us with all wisdom and understanding" (Ephesians 1:7-8). While our journey to wisdom begins with our belief in Jesus Christ, it continues to grow as our relationship deepens into true intimacy with Him. Paul prayed for the Ephesians, "I keep asking that the God of our Lord Jesus Christ, the glorious Father, may give you the Spirit of wisdom and revelation, so that you may know him better" (Ephesians 1:17).

God is the One who gives us wisdom, but we play a role in the impartation as well. He speaks to us though the pages of the Bible, through prayer, and through the power of the Holy Spirit.

The Bible. "All Scripture is God-breathed and is useful for teaching, rebuking, correcting and training in righteousness, so that the man of God may be thoroughly equipped for every good work" (2 Timothy 3:16-17).

Prayer. "If any of you lacks wisdom, He should ask God, who gives generously to all without finding fault, and it will be given to him" (James 1:5).

Holy Spirit. "The Spirit searches all things, even the deep things of God. For who among men knows the thoughts of a man except the man's spirit within him? In the same way no one knows the thoughts of God except the Spirit of God. We have not received the spirit of the world but the Spirit who is from God, that we may understand what God has freely given us. This is what we speak, not in words taught us by human wisdom but in words taught by the Spirit, expressing spiritual truths in spiritual words" (1 Corinthians 3:10-13).

God also pours wisdom into our lives through wise people. Solomon warned, "He who walks with the wise grows wise, but a companion of fools suffers harm" (Proverbs 13:20). That is why it is so important to have friends who speak wisdom and not foolishness. Their words will be absorbed into your spirit, and the next thing you know...out pops foolishness from your own mouth.

What does wise speech sound like? James explains: "The wisdom that comes from heaven is first of all pure; then peace-loving, considerate, submissive, full of mercy and good fruit, impartial and sincere" (James 3:17).

My husband's Aunt Iris was one of the wisest women I've ever known. She never conjugated a Greek or Hebrew verb or earned a college degree. But she knew God and immersed herself in His presence continually. I'd often hear her singing, "I come to the garden alone, while the dew is still on the roses…And He walks with me, and He talks with me, and He tells me I am his own; and the joy we share as we tarry there, none other has ever known." Iris was a wise woman.

I believe wisdom has little to do with intelligence. When it comes to applying wise principles to the words we speak or don't speak, I like what Frank M. Garafda had to say: "The difference between a smart man (woman) and a wise man (woman) is that a smart man (woman) knows what to say, and a wise man (woman) knows whether to say it or not."

I have known many highly educated fools. Apparently, so did the apostle Paul. He wrote, "Do not deceive yourselves. If any one of you thinks he is wise by the standards of this age, he should become a 'fool' so that he may become wise. For the wisdom of this world is foolishness in God's sight" (1 Corinthians 3:18-19).

There is nothing wrong with knowledge, but there is a vast difference between wisdom and knowledge. Wisdom is the God-given ability to apply knowledge correctly. "A wise person makes decisions based on the understanding that God and his time-honored principles are the only sure foundation for life. A foolish person does not act on the foundation of a reverence for God and instead lives recklessly for selfish gain."[2]

"Like a gold ring in a pig's snout is a beautiful woman who knows no discretion" (Proverbs 11:22). I call that the original Miss Piggy. No matter how beautiful a woman is on the outside, a lack of discretion in her vocabulary will mar the view.

Here's a general rule of thumb: If in doubt, leave it out. In other words, if you are not sure if you should say something, then don't.

Suppose God came to you in a dream and said, "Ask for whatever you want Me to give you." What would you say? Young King Solomon had a ready answer…wisdom. Dear sister, there is only one way to know when to speak and when to be silent—by becoming a wise godly woman. "By wisdom a house is built, and through understanding it is established; through knowledge its rooms are filled with rare and beautiful treasures" (Proverbs 24:3-4).

Timing Is Crucial

When Steven was about seven years old, we went snow skiing. For hours I instructed him in how to stand up, ski down, and get up once he fell. In his frustration, Steven fell down and fell down and fell down. He was not getting the hang of it at all. *What's the problem,* I wondered. Then I found out. It was me.

"Mom," Steven cried, "if you just quit telling me what to do, I think I could get it."

"Fine!" I said. "Go ahead and do it your way!"

And you know what? He did. Thirty minutes later Steven was cruising down the slopes with ease. My continued instruction had been a hindrance to Steven working out the maneuvers on his own. It started out being a skiing lesson for Steven, but it ended up being a parenting lesson for me.

> *I seldom feel sorry for the things I did not say.*
>
> —AUTHOR UNKNOWN

Sometimes the most powerful words are the ones we withhold. "There is a time for everything and a season for every activity under heaven...a time to be silent and a time to speak" (Ecclesiastes 3:1,7).

In the Bible, Esther is a wonderful example of a wise woman who knew that timing was crucial. After much prayer, fasting, and deliberation, she went before the king to make a petition. It was an important request because the entire Hebrew nation was at stake. Rather than grovel at the king's feet in dismay, she calmly invited him to dinner. When the king attended the soiree the following evening, once again he invited Esther to make her request. Once again, she invited him to dinner the following evening.

At the second dinner party, the king offered yet a third opportunity for Esther to make her request. Finally, Esther revealed evil Haman's plot to annihilate the entire Hebrew nation, which included her life as well. It is an amazing story, and I encourage you to read the book of Esther. But here's a lesson among the drama. Esther had a very important request for the king. And yet it was all about timing. Sure, she could have made the request the first time she approached the king and he extended the golden scepter in approval. She could have offered her petition at the first dinner party when he offered her anything she desired, "up to half the kingdom" (Esther 5:3). But there was something in Esther's spirit that caused her to wait. The timing wasn't right.

Even though the Bible doesn't tell us directly, I believe Esther was listening to God. Because of her obedience, the entire Hebrew nation was saved. That is the power of a woman's words offered at the right time.

A large part of discerning when to be silent and when to speak is learning how to listen well. "Listening is midwifery, the work of someone willing to allow another to labor in pain and joy, who refuses to numb these precious things by coming too quickly to reassure or make everything right. Listening to another person enables, gently facilitates birth...to help another who has lost hope to come to light through the process."[3]

It may be easier to anesthetize the patient and forcefully pull the baby from the womb, but that is not usually the healthiest course of action. The Bible teaches:

- [She] who guards her lips guards [her] life, but [she] who speaks rashly will come to ruin (Proverbs 13:3).

- Do you see a [woman] who speaks in haste? There is more hope for a fool than for [her] (Proverbs 29:20).

- [She] who answers before listening—that is [her] folly and [her] shame (Proverbs 18:13).

- Everyone should be quick to listen, slow to speak and slow to become angry, for [woman's] anger does not bring about the righteous life that God desires (James 1:19-20).

Ralph Waldo Emerson said, "A friend is a person with whom I may be sincere. Before him, I may think aloud." In order to think aloud, someone has to be on the receiving end listening. There is a difference between truly listening and waiting for your turn to talk. A true listener...

- Does not interrupt. Interrupting communicates, "What I have to say is more important than what you have to say."

- Invites you to tell her more with words such as, "How did that make you feel?"

- Affirms the speaker with words such as, "Yes, I see." A true listener pays attention not only to the words of the speaker, but also to the emotions that drive the words.

- Does not offer a solution unless asked. "What you should do is..." This minimizes the person's problems and makes it appear that you have all the answers. In other words, the person feels worse than before they confided the problem.

- Does not judge. For example, "That was a terrible way to act."

- Does not argue. It is better to be kind than correct when listening to someone pour out her heart.

- Listens for the emotions behind the words in addition to the words themselves. "That must have been painful for you."

In Dietrich Bonhoeffer's classic work *Life Together,* he wrote this about the ministry of listening:

The first service that one owes to others in the fellowship consists in listening to them. Just as love of God begins with listening to His Word, so the beginning of love for the brethren is learning to listen to them. It is God's love for us that He not only gives us His Word but also lends us His ear. So it is His work that we do for our brother when we learn to listen to him. Christians…forget that listening can be a greater service than speaking.

Many people are looking for an ear that will listen. They do not find it among Christians, because these Christians are talking when they should be listening. But he who can no longer listen to his brother will soon no longer be listening to God either; he will be doing nothing but prattle in the presence of God too. Anyone who thinks that his time is too valuable to spend keeping quiet will eventually have no time for God and his brother, but only for himself and his own follies.[4]

Jesus was a master listener. He never interrupted but asked good questions that helped people come to their own conclusions. He listened to the lame man lying by the pool, the leper languishing by the side of the road, the children clamoring around His feet, the desperate father pleading for his child's sanity, the friend questioning His true identity, and His Father giving Him daily instructions.

Some of the most poignant moments of Jesus' arrest were the silent ones. "He was oppressed and afflicted, yet he did not open his mouth; he was led like a lamb to the slaughter, and as a sheep before her shearers is silent, so he did not open his mouth" (Isaiah 53:7). And for you and me, some of our most powerful moments will be the ones in which we remain silent. Some of the most powerful words are the ones that are withheld.

*T*HE *P*ASSPORT TO *R*EFRESHING THE *S*OUL

Come to me, all you who are weary and burdened,
and I will give you rest. Take my yoke upon you and learn from me,
for I am gentle and humble in heart, and you will find rest for
your souls. For my yoke is easy and my burden is light.

—MATTHEW 11:28-30

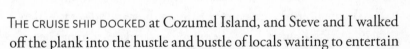

THE CRUISE SHIP DOCKED at Cozumel Island, and Steve and I walked off the plank into the hustle and bustle of locals waiting to entertain the new batch of tourists entering their bit of paradise.

"Let's get away from all the congestion," Steve suggested. "I want to see the unspoiled part of the island."

So we rented a small motorcycle, donned our helmets, and set out on an adventure.

"This road goes around the island," the renter explained. "Just stay on this road and you will return."

Off we went to circle the beautiful island of Cozumel. It wasn't too long before civilization lay behind and the open road promised romantic scenery. Deserted white sandy beaches hugged the road on the right. But after several miles, the landscape changed. Lush palms transformed into bare craggy branches. Seagulls were replaced with dark menacing vultures, and the terrain was piled high with debris. No longer was this a peaceful ride through paradise. We were lone travelers on the back side of the island, and we suddenly realized we were unprotected prey for any number of predators watching for unsuspecting tourists who had lost their way. The stench of the island's landfill assaulted our senses, and the circling birds of prey seemed waiting for our demise.

"Can't this thing go any faster?" I asked.

"I've got it wide open," Steve assured. "I'm trying to get us out of here as fast as I can."

I am delighted to report that we did make it back to civilization. We threw off those helmets and ran across the plank to the ship as fast as our shaky legs could take us. In a matter of three hours, we had gone full circle. Paradise, garbage heap, paradise.

Why do I tell you this story? Because there are some days when I feel as though I am on the back side of the island. I look around and there is garbage everywhere. I sense vultures circling the air just waiting for me to fall so they can pick me apart. The breeze is filled with stench, and paradise is filled with parasites.

I cry, "How can I be a vessel to empower other people with the words of my mouth? I am empty! I am on the back side of the island! I have nothing to give! I am the one who needs encouragement!"

As I thought about the days when I feel as though I have nothing to give—that I am the one who needs a kind word, I realize I am not the only person who has ever felt that way. King David had many days when he felt as though he were on the back side of the island.

God Refreshes David

While King Saul was still on his throne, God chose David to be Saul's successor. This didn't sit too well with the king, and he attempted to kill David before the crown could be placed on his handsome head. The young David, who earlier had bravely charged the Philistine giant Goliath, now ran for his life. The one place Saul didn't think David would hide was among the Philistines, whom he had previously shamed. So that is exactly where David hid...the briar patch, so to speak.

By this time David had a 600-man army gathered round him. Each man brought his wife and children to live in the camp. The ragtag team of outcasts became David's kingdom for a time.

One day while David and his men were off fighting a battle, another group of people, the Amalekites, invaded their camp and took their wives and children captive. When David and his men returned home, they found empty beds, smoldering fires, and the haunting absence of familiar voices.

The men wept until they had no more tears or energy for recourse. Rather than devise a rescue plan, they turned their anger on their leader and threatened to stone him. Hurting people often hurt people, and they were looking for someone to blame.

Can you imagine how David must have felt? His previous employer was trying to kill him (he had worked in Saul's palace), his best friends had turned against him, and his wife and children had been taken captive or possibly killed. Where was he to turn? How could he encourage his men when he had nothing left to give?

There was only one place to turn...to God.

"David found strength in the LORD his God" (1 Samuel 30:6). Friend, sometimes to God is the only place we have to go. Isn't it a shame that we wait until God is our last resort rather than our first line of defense? Yes, God has called us to live in community with other believers, but sometimes I believe He wants us all to Himself.

Moses was alone with God when he talked to Him in the burning bush. Hagar was alone with God when He spoke to her and gave her water in the desert. Elijah was alone with God when God revealed Himself in the still, small voice. Jesus often went away by Himself to commune with His Father. Where do we go when we feel that we have nothing to give? Where do we go when we are the ones who need an encouraging word?

When we feel that we are on the back side of the island, we need to make sure we don't get off the motorcycle and park by the garbage heap. Keep going! Begin using your words to praise God and fuel the vehicle that will get you out of the dumps.

Praise Refreshes the Soul

One day I was mopping the kitchen floor and my words were anything but cheerful. I grumbled to myself, *No one appreciates all I do around here. All I ever do is clean, clean, clean.* Then God began to whisper a new thought to my heart. *Suppose you were blind and couldn't see the beautiful patterns on the linoleum floor, or the spilled juice by the refrigerator, or the crumbs under the baby's chair? If you were deaf, you couldn't hear the soothing sound of the soap bubbles dissolving in the scrub bucket. You couldn't hear the rhythmic sound of the mop being pushed back and forth across the floor's hard surface. Suppose you were confined to a wheelchair and not strong enough to stand upright and grasp the wooden handle to erase the muddy footprints and make the floor shiny and clean again? Suppose you didn't have a home or a family to clean up after?*

> The Sovereign LORD has given me an instructed tongue, to know the word that sustains the weary.
>
> —ISAIAH 50:4

These thoughts brought a new perspective to this mundane task, and my grumblings turned into a prayer of thanksgiving. I stood up straight, proudly grasped the mop, and began to pray. *Thank You, Lord, for the privilege of mopping this dirty floor. Thank You for the health and strength to hold this mop, for the ability to wrap my agile fingers around its handle and feel the wood in my hands. Thank You for the sight to see the crumbs and the dirt, for the sense of smell to enjoy the clean scent of the soap in my bucket. Thank You for the precious feet that will walk through this room and dirty it again. Those feet are the reason I do this job. And, Lord, thank You for the privilege of having a floor to mop and a family to clean up after.*

Oh, yes. It's marvelous how a godly perspective can change our attitudes and the words that reflect them. When we begin to praise God in the middle of the mundane, He refreshes us with a new outlook on life! The book of Psalms is a powerful collection of praises to God, and interestingly, many of the beautiful verses were written when David was struggling with depression, desperation, or devastation. Let's take a look at a few.

> O LORD, how many are my foes! How many rise up against me! Many are saying of me, "God will not deliver him." But you are a shield around me, O LORD; you bestow glory on me and lift up my head (Psalm 3:1-4).

> Answer me when I call to you, O my righteous God. Give me relief from my distress; be merciful to me and hear my prayer...You have filled my heart with greater joy than when their grain and new wine abound. I will lie down and sleep in peace, for you alone, O LORD, make me dwell in safety (Psalm 4:1,7-8).

When you are discouraged, try praising God. There is an old hymn that says "Count your blessings, name them one by one, count your blessings, see what God hath done!"

I believe we tend to remember what we need to forget and forget what we need to remember. When we remember the blessings, we are reminded of God's faithfulness and tender care. The remembering will help fill us up when we feel our emotional tank is running low.

"David found strength in the LORD." Sooner or later we all come to a point where we feel alone and discouraged—when people are simply not enough. That's when we need God to wrap us in His loving arms.

Jesus experienced that on many occasions. On the night before

His arrest, He left the company of His closest friends and "going a little farther, he fell with his face to the ground and prayed" (Matthew 26:39). At that point, Jesus needed more than His friends. He needed His Dad. Likewise, there will be times when we are desperate and the words of mere humans are not enough. We need to go to a deeper place, a place alone with God, and let His words encourage us.

Refreshing Others Will Bring Refreshment to You

A sign was posted on a telephone pole by the grocery store: "LOST DOG with three legs, blind in left eye, missing right ear, tail broken, and recently castrated. Answers to the name of Lucky!"

Perhaps as you've been reading about the power of a woman's words and the incredible ability we have to change the course of a day or a life by the words we speak, you've thought...*I'm the one who needs encouraging! How can I pour life into someone else when I feel dead on the inside? How can I offer a cup of encouragement when I am bone dry with nothing left to give?* Perhaps you feel just about as fortunate as the lost dog named Lucky.

There was a woman in the Bible who also felt that she had nothing left to give, but God showed her how to fill her cup. The story is found in 1 Kings 17.

Elijah was a good prophet who gave some bad news to a king named Ahab: "As the LORD, the God of Israel, lives, whom I serve, there will be neither dew nor rain in the next few years except at my word" (1 Kings 17:1). God knew that news would not go over very well with the king, so He told Elijah to flee eastward and hide in the Kerith Ravine east of the Jordan. For several months Elijah drank from the brook and ate bread and meat delivered by ravens that God miraculously sent to feed him. Only kings could afford to eat meat every day; God provided the very best for His servant.

Sometime later the brook dried up. Now, if God could supply meat and bread every day, He could have easily provided water. But God had a different idea. He sent Elijah to Zarephath to a Gentile widow who needed a miracle in her life.

Elijah did as the Lord said and traveled to this widow's home. But he didn't find a woman with abundance ready to provide sustenance. What he found was a widow who had given up on life and felt as though she had nothing left to give. When he arrived, she was stooping to the ground picking up sticks and placing them in a bundle.

"Excuse me," Elijah called, "could you please bring me a cup of water?"

As she turned to get the traveler a cup to quench his thirst, he continued. "Oh, and can you bring me a piece of bread?"

With this request, I imagine the woman sarcastically grumbled, *And would you like a lamb chop to go along with it?*

"I don't have any bread—only a handful of flour in a jar and a little oil in a jug," she said. "I am gathering a few sticks to take home and make a meal for myself and my son, that we may eat it—and die" (1 Kings 17:12).

Now that was a discouraged woman! But Elijah had good news for her.

"Don't be afraid," Elijah said. "Go home and do as you have said. But first make a small cake of bread for me from what you have and bring it to me, and then make something for yourself and your son. For this is what the LORD, the God of Israel says: 'The jar of flour will not be used up and the jug of oil will not run dry until the day the LORD gives rain on the land'" (verses 13-14).

She went away and did what Elijah had told her.

Can't you just see this woman taking the last bit of flour and oil to make Elijah a meal? *What does it matter? I'm going to die anyway. So what if it is one day early.*

She emptied her flour bowl and oil jar, took a little cake to Elijah, and returned home. As she goes to wash the dirty dishes, she picks up the jar and the jug and her senses are jostled! The jar is full of flour and the jug is full to the brim with oil. She was an empty woman, but as she took what little she had to offer encouragement to another, God filled her up.

I call this the Bucket Principle. I believe that each of us is given a bucket of encouragement that we are to pour onto those around us. As we dip out of our bucket and pour onto others, God miraculously fills it back up.

There are those who have buckets that are running a bit low or even close to empty. Maybe they haven't had many deposits from other people lately, or maybe their bucket has a leak. In order to try to fill their bucket, they dip out of someone else's bucket with a cutting word here or a degrading comment there. But you know what? You can never get your bucket filled by dipping out of someone else's. You can only get your bucket filled by dipping out of your own and sharing the encouragement with others. When you give from your bucket of encouragement, God is there to pour more back into you. After Naomi had lost her husband and her two sons, she said, "I went away full, but the LORD has brought me back empty" (Ruth 1:21). What she did not realize was that He had provided Ruth to dip out of her bucket to fill Naomi's up again. In the meantime, God kept Ruth's filled to the brim. He filled Naomi's bucket, He filled the widow's bucket, and He will fill yours as well.

> *I have many times been driven to my knees by the utter conviction that I had nowhere else to go.*
>
> —ABRAHAM LINCOLN

Jesus said, "Give, and it will be given to you. A good measure, pressed down, shaken together and running over, poured into your lap. For with the measure you use, it will be measured to you" (Luke 6:38). Many times we place a lid on our bucket of encouragement. *I don't have enough to give to someone else. I am drained dry,* we lament. However, when we give, even in our emotional emptiness, God fills us back up.

He also taught, "Remember this: Whoever sows sparingly will also reap sparingly, and whoever sows generously will also reap generously" (2 Corinthians 9:6). Do you want your bucket of encouragement and positive words to be filled to overflowing? Then begin dipping out and pouring into the lives of others. The same Jesus who multiplied five loaves of bread and two tiny fish into a feast to feed 5000 men plus women and children (Matthew 14:15-21) will take your simple words of encouragement and multiply them to feed *your* hungry soul.

We play a game with our friends called Shanghai. Each player is dealt 11 cards and the object of the game is to play your cards on other players' cards. While most games are about accumulating points, in this game the first person to give all the cards away wins.

That's how it is with the game of life. The more encouraging words you give away, the more you win! Some words are people specific, but some are wild cards and can be played anywhere. "Thank you," "Please," "I'm sorry," "You did that so well," "I appreciate that." These are wild cards that will brighten anyone's day. Go ahead. Try it. You'll be amazed at the power you have to change the course of a day.

What happened to the woman from Zarephath? "For the jar of flour was not used up and the jug of oil did not run dry, in keeping with the word of the LORD spoken by Elijah" (1 Kings 17:16).

Refreshing Others Through Written Words

There is great power in the words that come out of our mouths, but the written word is also a powerful tool when it comes to refreshing others. On many occasions a timely note of encouragement has given me the push I needed to continue on.

When my son was in the seventh grade, he was taking advanced math, advanced English, advanced science, and Latin. It was also his first year playing on a school sports team, and he got home about 6:00 at night. Nothing was going well. It was hard to get his schoolwork done when he came home exhausted each evening. A few times he had worked hard on an assignment, only to find that he had done the wrong page. Latin was Greek to him, and there was no sign that he was going to catch on anytime soon.

One day after practice, I heard him in the shower crying out to God. "Lord, I'm not good at anything. Just help me be good at something. Just one thing."

That broke my heart. Actually, Steven was great at many things, but his emotions and workload were too much to bear. I met with the principal and we dropped one of the advanced courses (Latin), but his year really turned around with a written note from one of his teachers, who knew he was struggling and needed an extra pat on the back. In it she wrote:

> Dear Mr. and Mrs. Jaynes,
>
> Steven has been doing excellent work in science. His name has been at the top of the list on recent tests and quizzes. No doubt he told you about his perfect score on our last test. He is a fine young man. I would love a room full of Stevens!
>
> Best regards,
>
> Mrs. Connie Roads

Though this note of encouragement was addressed to Steven's dad and me, in reality it was for our son. Mrs. Roads is a very wise woman who looked past the tough exterior of adolescence and saw a wavering heart. It was the turning point of our son's year. She gave Steven the refreshment he needed in her written words, and he was ready to stay the course and finish well.

Oh, friend, we have so much power in our words. Whether they are spoken through the lips of a wise woman or penned by the hand of a willing writer, our words can be the passport to refresh the weary and get them off the back side of the island and back onto the road of paradise. Our words can change the course of a life.

THE *P*ROFOUND *P*OSSIBILITIES

*The tongue of a man (woman) is his (her) sword
and affective speech stronger than all fighting.*

—AUTHOR UNKNOWN

LISTEN...DO YOU HEAR THEM? Open your front door and step out into the world. They swarm around and surround us on every side. Small ones with tremendous impact. Large ones looming and misunderstood. Swirling. Churning. Spinning. Burning. Listen, do you hear them? One of the mightiest forces in all creation...words.

God has given each of us a priceless gift with profound possibilities to impact the world we live in for good. How will we use this gift? How will our words be received?

An artist discovered the profound possibilities he possessed as he painted the portrait of a homeless man. He came to the park every day at the same time, when the light was just right, positioning his easel and paints under the same familiar shade tree. It was his favorite spot to work and the perfect setting in which to satisfy his passion for painting. A talented and sensitive man, he specialized in portraits, skillfully drawing out the inner qualities of his subject. He watched the people strolling by for hours, searching for just the right face to paint. He loved the way each face told many different stories; some were filled with joy and others with pain and sadness, but all were filled with life.

A homeless man sitting across the path caught the artist's eye. Thinking of God's handiwork in every human being, he resolved to paint the man as he imagined he could be. With the last stroke, he breathed a sign of satisfaction, a contented smile spreading across his face. It was done. And it was some of his best work. The artist then called the man over to see the painting. "Is this me?" the homeless man asked. "That is the 'you' I see!" replied the artist. The man stared at the painting silently. Finally, with tears in his eyes, he softly declared, "If that's the man you see in me, then that's the man I'm going to be!"[1]

Each and every day we are painting portraits of the people we meet. We may not be holding a paintbrush and splashing brilliant colors on canvas, but we are painting pictures with the words we speak. Men, women, boys, and girls are seeing themselves in our words. Many are determining their worth, their potential, and even their destiny by what they hear others say about them.

Will your words reflect the fact that each individual is "God's masterpiece" (Ephesians 2:10 NLT), "chosen...and dearly loved" (Colossians 3:12), "fearfully and wonderfully made" (Psalm 139:14)? You have that potential, you know. It's right under your nose.

You Are Becoming Whom You Are Going to Be

So here we are at the end of our journey and the question remains, how will we use our words...one of God's most incredible gifts to mankind. Will we invest them wisely or squander them foolishly? Will we use them to build up others or tear them down? Oh, the power we possess to bless those around us and encourage them to be all that God has created them to be. Our very words have the potential to change the course of a day...to change the course of a life.

Day by day we are becoming whom we are going to be. Let me close with words that have had a great impact on my life as I ponder the future and the woman who will one day look back at me in the mirror.

You'll Meet an Old Lady One Day

You are going to meet an old lady someday. Down the road 10, 20, 30 years—she's waiting for you. You will catch up to her. What kind of old lady are you going to meet?

She may be a seasoned, soft, and gracious lady. A lady who has grown old gracefully, surrounded by a host of friends—friends who call her blessed because of what her life has meant to them. Or she may be a bitter, disillusioned, dried-up, cynical old buzzard without a good word for anyone or anything—soured, friendless, and alone. The kind of old lady you will meet will depend entirely upon you.

She will be exactly what you make of her, nothing more, nothing less. It's up to you. You will have no one else to credit or blame. Every day, in every way, you are becoming more and more like that old lady. You are getting to look more like her, think more like her, and talk more like her. You are becoming her. If you live only in terms of what you are getting out of life, the old lady gets smaller, drier, harder, crabbier, more self-centered. Open your life to others. Think in terms of what you can give and your contribution to life, and the old lady grows larger, softer, kinder, greater.

These little things, seemingly so unimportant now—attitudes, goals, ambitions, desires—are adding up inside where you cannot see them, crystallizing in your heart and mind. The point is, these things don't always show up immediately. But they will—sooner than you think. Someday they will harden into that old lady; nothing will be able to soften or change them then.

The time to take care of that old lady is right now. Today. Examine your motives, attitudes, goals. Check up on her. Work her over now while she is still pliable, still in a formative condition. Then you will be much more likely to meet a lovely, gracious old lady at the proper time.[2]

Notes

Chapter 2—God's Incredible Gift

1. "Three Letters from Teddy," by Elizabeth Silance Ballard. From *Home Life,* March 1976. Copyright 1976 by the Sunday School Board of the Southern Baptist Convention (now LifeWay Christian Resources of the Southern Baptist Convention). All rights reserved. Used by permission from the author.

2. <www.en.wikipedia.org/wiki/wildfire.>

3. Spiros Zodhiates, as quoted in *The Tale of the Tardy Ox Cart,* compiled by Charles Swindoll (Nashville, TN: Word Publishing, 1998), p. 575.

4. Charles Swindoll, *Encourage Me* (Grand Rapids, MI: Zondervan Publishing House, 1992), p. 19.

5. William Barclay, "The Letter to the Hebrews," *The Daily Study Bible* (Edinburgh, Scotland: St. Andrews Press, 1955), pp. 173-78.

6. Adapted from Sister Helen P. Mrosla, O.S.F., "All the Good Things." Originally published in *Proteus,* Spring 1991. Reprinted by permission as edited and published by *Reader's Digest* in October 1991.

Chapter 3—A Woman's Amazing Potential

1. Copyright © by Jean Harper. Used by permission.

2. Alan Loy McGinnis, *Bringing Out the Best in People* (Minneapolis, MN: Augsburg Publishing House, 1985), pp. 71-72.

3. Carolyn's story is found in *Treasures of Encouragement* by Sharon W. Betters (Phillipsburg, NJ: P&R Publishing, 1996), pp. 160-61.

4. Adapted from "Chosen," by James Scott and Marie Curling in *Stories from the Heart,* compiled by Alice Gray (Sisters, OR: Multnomah Publishers, 1996), p. 37.

5. Adapted from "When a Stranger Called, He Answered," by Mark Washburn, *The Charlotte Observer,* page E1, December 9, 2006.

Chapter 4—The Power of a Woman's Words to Children

1. "Mama's Plan," is reprinted with permission from *Guideposts* magazine. Copyright © 1988 by Guideposts, Carmel, NY 10512. All rights reserved. <www.guidepostsmag.com>.

2. Neil Anderson, *Victory Over the Darkness* (Ventura, CA: Regal Books, 1990), p. 63.

3. William Barclay, "Letters to the Galatians and Ephesians," *The Daily Study Bible* (Edinburgh, Scotland: St. Andrews Press, 1962), p. 211.

4. Karol Ladd, *The Power of a Positive Mom* (West Monroe, LA: Howard Publishing Co., Inc., 2001).

5. Ibid., p. 41.

6. Mabel Bartlett and Sophia Baker, *Mothers—Makers of Men* (New York, NY: Exposition Press, 1952), p. 92.

7. "I Don't Believe a Word of It" from Alice Gray, *More Stories for the Heart* (Sisters, OR: Multnomah Publishers, 1997), p. 46.

Chapter 5—The Power of a Woman's Words to Her Husband

1. Carolyn Custis James, *When Life and Beliefs Collide* (Grand Rapids, MI: Zondervan Publishing House, 2001), p. 181.

2. Nancy Anderson, "I Am a Woman—Hear Me Roar" copyright © 2004 <www.nancyCanderson.com>. Used by permission.

3. From the Billy Graham Evangelistic Association, *Billy Graham, God's Ambassador* (Nashville, TN: Word Publishing Group, 1999).

4. Ibid.

5. <www.bgea.org/News_Article.asp?ArticleID=163>.

6. Taken from Ed Wheat, *Love Life for Every Couple* (Grand Rapids, MI: Zondervan Publishing House, 1980), p. 177.

7. Excerpted from Sharon Jaynes, *Becoming the Woman of His Dreams* (Eugene, OR: Harvest House Publishers, 2005), pp. 42-44, 69-73.

8. Jack Cranfield and Mark Victor Hansen, "Encouragement," from *Chicken Soup for the Soul* (Deerfield Beach, FL: Health Communications, Inc., 1993), p. 213.

Chapter 6—The Power of a Woman's Words to Her Friends

1. Charles Caldwell Ryrie, *Ryrie Study Bible* (Chicago, IL: Moody Publishers, 1977), p. 1778.

2. Ann Hibbard, *Treasured Friends* (Grand Rapids, MI: Baker Books, 1997), pp. 16-17.

Chapter 7—The Power of a Woman's Words to Fellow Believers

1. Kenneth Barker, general ed., *NIV Study Bible* (Grand Rapids, MI: Zondervan Publishing House, 1995), p. 336.

2. Kenneth L. Barker and John R. Kohlenberger III, *Zondervan NIV Commentary Volume 1: Old Testament* (Grand Rapids, MI: Zondervan Publishing House, 1994), p. 198.

3. Robert J. Moran, *Nelson's Complete Book of Stories, Illustrations, and Quotes* (Nashville, TN: Thomas Nelson, 2000), p. 122.

4. Kenneth W. Osbeck, *101 Hymn Stories* (Grand Rapids, MI: Kregel Publications, 1982), pp. 43-44.

Chapter 8—The Power of a Woman's Words to the World

1. Adapted from Dan Clark, "Are You God?" in *Chicken Soup for the Woman's Soul* (Deerfield Beach, FL: Health Communications, Inc., 1996), p. 27.

2. Alan Loy McGinnis, *The Friendship Factor* (Minneapolis, MN: Augsburg Publishing House, 1979), pp. 101-02.

3. David Jeremiah, *The Power of Encouragement* (Sisters, OR: Multnomah Publishers, 1997), p. 13.

4. Richard H. Seume, *Shoes for the Road* (Chicago, IL: Moody Press, 1974), p. 117.

Chapter 9—The Power of a Woman's Words to God

1. Kenneth L. Barker and John R. Kohlenberger III, *Zondervan NIV Commentary Volume 1: Old Testament* (Grand Rapids, MI: Zondervan Publishing House, 1994), p. 38.

2. Sharon Jaynes, *Being a Great Mom, Raising Great Kids* (Chicago, IL: Moody Publishers, 2000), pp. 41-43.

3. James Strong, *The New Strong's Exhaustive Concordance of the Bible* (Nashville, TN: Thomas Nelson, 1990), p. 68.

4. Ibid., p. 8.

5. Sharon W. Betters, *Treasures of Encouragement* (Phillipsburg, NJ: P&R Publishing, 1996), p. 9.

6. Ibid., p. 150.

7. G. Campbell Morgan, *The Practice of Prayer* (New York, NY: Revel, 1960; Grand Rapids, MI: Baker, 1971), pp. 125-26.

Chapter 10—The Promise of Power

1. Joann C. Webster and Karen Davis, eds., *A Celebration of Women* (Southlake, TX: Watercolor Books, 2001), p. 167.

2. Kenneth L. Barker and John R. Kohlenberger III, *Zondervan NIV Commentary Volume 1: Old Testament* (Grand Rapids, MI: Zondervan Publishing House, 1994), p. 1290

3. Alan Loy McGinnis, *Bringing Out the Best in People* (Minneapolis, MN: Augsburg Publishing House, 1985), p. 48.

Chapter 11—The Product of Practice

1. W.E. Vine, Merrill F. Unger, and William White Jr., *Vine's Complete Expository Dictionary of Old and New Testament Words* (Nashville, TN: Thomas Nelson Publishers, 1985), p. 26.

2. Corrie ten Boom with Jamie Buckingham, *Tramp for the Lord* (Old Tappan, NJ: Revell Company, 1974), p. 12.

Chapter 12—The Potency of Silence

1. Charles L. Allen, *God's Psychiatry* (Grand Rapids, MI: Fleming H. Revell Company, 1953), p. 75.

2. Karol Ladd, *The Power of a Positive Woman* (West Monroe, LA: Howard Publishing Co., Inc., 2002), p. 75.

3. Marlee Alex, "An Open Window," *Virtue* (May/June 1994), p. 4.

4. Dietrich Bonhoeffer, *Life Together,* trans. John W. Doberstein (New York, NY: Harper & Brothers, 1954), pp. 97-98.

Chapter 14—The Profound Possibilities

1. Mary Southerland, *Sandpaper People* (Eugene, OR: Harvest House Publishers, 2005), pp. 13-14.

2. Author Unknown.

Dig Deeper to Find New Strength in Your Voice in

*T*HE POWER OF A WOMAN'S WORDS WORKBOOK AND STUDY GUIDE

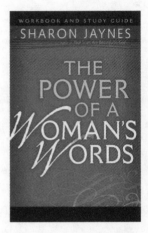

Words are one of the most powerful forces in the universe, yet God entrusts them to mere mortals. This in-depth Bible study takes a closer look at what God has to say about our words. Popular author and speaker Sharon Jaynes spends time with several women in the Bible to discover the lasting impact their words had on those around them, and how those words have lingering effects even today.

- How did Rachel's words affect her son's character?
- How did Delilah's words affect her husband's future?
- How did Elizabeth's words affect her friend's confidence?

This easy-to-use guide provides opportunities for both study and reflection to bring about lasting change in your life. The chapters follow the chapters in *The Power of a Woman's Words* and are perfect for individual or group study.

Other Books By Sharon Jaynes

YOUR SCARS ARE BEAUTIFUL TO GOD
Sharon shares with women how emotional scars can lead to healing and restoration. Encouraging chapters and inspirational stories reveal how you can give your past pains over to the One who turns hurts into hope and heartache into happiness.

BUILDING AN EFFECTIVE WOMEN'S MINISTRY
This unique yet practical how-to manual offers a wide range of help to women, from those just starting out to those who have a thriving ministry but could use a fresh idea or two. For groups large and small, this is a treasure trove of detailed information on how to serve and care for women.

BECOMING THE WOMAN OF HIS DREAMS
Sharon provides a thoughtful look at the wonderful, unique, and God-ordained role a woman has in her husband's life. If you would like a little "wow!" back in your relationship with the man you married, let seven simple secrets, biblical wisdom, and tender stories of both men and women inspire you to truly be the wife your husband longs for.

BECOMING A WOMAN WHO LISTENS TO GOD
"When I pour over the pages of Scripture," says Sharon, "I discover that some of God's most memorable messages were not delivered while men and women were away on a spiritual retreat, but right in the middle of the hustle and bustle of everyday life. He spoke to Moses while he was tending sheep, to Gideon while he was threshing wheat, to the woman at the well while she was drawing water for her housework. It is not a matter of does He speak, but will we listen." Discover with Sharon what it means to become a woman who listens to God.

BECOMING SPIRITUALLY BEAUTIFUL
In *Becoming Spiritually Beautiful,* Sharon gently shares how becoming spiritually beautiful is something full of promise and possibilities. Readers will discover that true beauty is not based on external adornments—it's really all about what goes on inside a woman. In letting God transform their hearts, minds, wills, and emotions, women will see that knowing and loving the Lord is better than anything else.

HARVEST HOUSE PUBLISHERS

About the Author

Sharon Jaynes is an international inspirational speaker and Bible teacher for women's conferences and events. She is also the author of several books, including *Becoming the Woman of His Dreams, Becoming a Woman Who Listens to God, Experience the Ultimate Makeover,* and *Your Scars Are Beautiful to God.* Her books have been translated into several foreign languages and impacted women all around the globe. Sharon and her husband, Steve, live in North Carolina and have one grown son, Steven.

Sharon is always honored to hear from her readers. Please write to her directly at: *Sharon@sharonjaynes.com* or at her mailing address:

Sharon Jaynes
P.O. Box 725
Matthews, North Carolina 28106

To learn more about Sharon's books and speaking ministry or to inquire about having Sharon speak at your next event, visit

www.sharonjaynes.com.

HARVEST HOUSE PUBLISHERS